THE
DARKEST
HOUR

WHEN CRISIS STRIKES OUR LIVES

HIRAM DORADO

Library of Congress Control Number: 2019917389
ISBN: Hardcover   978-1-5065-3063-5
                   Softcover   978-1-5065-3065-9
                   eBook   978-1-5065-3064-2

Print information available on the last page.

Revision date: 26/11/2019

To order additional copies of this book, contact:
Palibrio
1663 Liberty Drive, Suite 200
Bloomington, IN 47403
Toll Free from the U.S.A 877.407.5847
Toll Free from Mexico 01.800.288.2243
Toll Free from Spain 900.866.949
From other International locations +1.812.671.9757
Fax: 01.812.355.1576
orders@palibrio.com
805029

CONTENTS

Author's Notes

This book, *The Darkest Hour*, is the new version of my previously printed book *The Midnight Hour*, published in 2012. The content of this book has a lot of personal experiences, advices, recommendations, warnings, and opinions. But by no means, I am declaring myself to be an expert on this subject. My constant burden to build healthy relationships has inspired me to reprint this book, and only with the assistance of all the books I have read and of all the experiences I have lived myself, I can speak about the seriousness of this subject and help others confront the most relevant issues that we face when crisis strike our own lives. But I will always encourage everyone to seek professional assistance when facing any personal crisis, and I will make an emphasis on the significance that we should never compare ourselves to others nor allow others to compare their unique circumstances to our own experiences since the intensity of pain, sorrow, grief, or misery is not the same for everyone, even if the circumstances appear to be very similar.

Preface

Don't feel strange if you find yourself reading this book while going through a personal crisis, neither will it be uncommon to be reading this book and your heart brings to mind a name of a person who may be needing some peer support or encouragement while the person is going through a personal crisis too.

And while we may be at either position of this predicament, whether we are appearing as the sufferer or as the encourager, our own personalities will always influence our minds to take certain inclinations. These inclinations will not help us at all if they bear any negative sentiment or wrong attitude but rather worsen our state of mind and make the darkest hour linger in our lives even longer. Although the chapters of this book will cover some of these inclinations, comparison, guiltiness, deception, self-punishment, unworthiness, insignificance, and so on, the most important forewarning that I must give before we start dealing with the whole process is to have an unprejudiced mind and an open heart to embrace the information and ideas I am sharing with you. Use these ideas, if they are of any value to you, to help you survive these overwhelming experiences, even if these ideas go against the major trends or most current developments.

Why am I suggesting that these ideas may go against these major trends? Well, we are living in times when every information we receive is constantly changing. But let me clear this personal point of view; I meant that one day, we may hear through the media about a certain product being harmful to our health, but few weeks later, we hear a contradictory explanation to that previous claim With this idea in mind, our own perception of different issues has been changing so fast with time, too, that we are now, for example, accepting stress as being part of our daily routines. So instead of evading certain events that bring anxiety, trauma, and tension to our personal lives, the major trends are now encouraging the public to accept such aggravated events as part of our existence. And I don't deny the fact that people could be in the right track, but our own tendency and the consequences after accepting this popular trend is that we will not have the patience and the tolerance to help those in need anymore. And if we do, we may judge their level of stress according to our own standards, assuming that their levels of stress are not as unbearable as they would have us believe and so should be more able to handle their own crises. Although on few occasions, this may be the truth, I do hope we can learn to establish a good perception so we are not drawn into more stress from those who don't like to help themselves. But needless to say, we are becoming more insensitive and impatient with ourselves and others because of how fast this world is constantly changing.

It is a fact that the way we are handling stress now is not how we used to handle stress years ago. Now, stress is being treated with destructive behaviors (by becoming compulsive buyers and developing obsessive consumer practices) instead of taking time to mediate or learning how to let go of things, people, and issues. But the most relevant consequence of our own perception about stress is that we are no longer considering stress as a life-threatening event. With so much advancement in medicine and all the available options we have to distract our minds, stress has become an issue that requires minimum attention.

This is why we are hearing people say things such as "It is only stress. Get over it" or "You shouldn't feel like that. I went through a more difficult situation than you did. You are just being weak" more often. We don't realize that we have become more complex individuals who cannot fit certain people in the same pattern as others or put one kind of people to a specific box or even place people in a box similar to where we put ourselves. For the sake of illustrating my point, let's take unhappiness. Being unhappy about something at work—which may appear insignificant to others—should have the same level of consideration or be taken as a life-threatening event as when pondering about another person's unhappiness, for example, of someone who may be going through a divorce. But the mainstream evaluates both cases against different standards without taking time to consider the level of stress, anxiety, or depression that each person could be going through. Another great example of wrong comparisons is the death of an animal companion. One stream may consider this type of death as irrelevant and insignificant when being compared to the death of a family member. This is why we must stop putting distinctions and comparisons among different types of life stressors that can have a big impact on the lives of people and even on our own.

Stress is stress. A lot of times stress is our normal reaction to how we handle changes—sometimes stress takes the best of us. We are all very different when dealing with a world that is constantly changing and has become more unstable. For these very reasons, I am reluctant to discriminate all the different crises we will face during our lifetime. Please understand that I am not minimizing a natural disaster, aggravated assaults, theft, rape, or any violence being done against you or a loved one or comparing anything less or anything more to sexual harassment or any other form of discrimination whether it was done against age, race, sexuality, etc. But rather, I am after the principle that can help everyone understand what tragedies, crises, and misfortunes mean to people so we can help them survive or help ourselves survive when these unpleasant events come to our lives. Understanding the process and properly dealing with the effects of our darkest hours will enable us to go through them with less struggle.

Introduction

I have purposely written this book to bring an understanding to the different transitions of seasons people go through during their darkest hours. This book may appear to be a little bit mystical, spiritual, or even weird at times because of its biblical language and all the examples or stories that are being used, but it still offers an accurate appreciation of all the personal crisis we can identify ourselves with.

It is my personal burden to illustrate this important subject. It is not an easy task, but it was born out of a desire to help people lessen their difficulties and those painful experiences that we all have to face during the different tragedies and crises life brings to us. Having experienced so many challenges myself, the motivation to share what I learned from those issues we normally deal with when facing all forms of grief ignited. At the same time, I saw a great need to provide more information about the darkest hours in our lives because there are very few books available pertaining to this subject.

Although there are so many movies and novels that make reference to this experiences as the dark night of the soul, the Christian Bible gives plenty of examples on what these darkest hours are all about. The Bible refers to these events as the midnight hours, which we will explain in future chapters. Many people have the tendency to see these distressful times as events that take place at precise and specific points in their lifetime, as if these times were already allocated by spiritual powers, divinely ascribed or astrologically irrevocable by the placement of the moon, stars, or the planets that govern their zodiac sign. All these ideas are bad information from people who are trying to intimidate and add more stress to society so their financial profits don't end. And I never have had any problem to state my unpleasant remarks to some of those religious centers and con artists who claim to know the future of our own fate and manipulate their limited ideas about God in order to keep people scared.

But the reason why the Bible gives so many examples about the midnight hours is because those were biblical periods of transition or portals that presented the potential or opportunity to break a person into a new season, and those new seasons often began in the darkest hours of the night. And that's exactly what takes place during our darkest hours too. When crisis strikes our lives, we also have the opportunity to break through a gate (or a portal). I think the best illustration of any darkest hour is when deep-sea divers immerse deep in the waters in search of pearls. Before they can enjoy the value and worth of those pearls, they must embrace the darkness of the waters, find those shells, and sensibly break them open. The *Midnight Hour* (being the original title of this manuscript), or *Darkest Hour* (as the new title), should be appreciated as those same defining moments that are critical and crucial in our lives that can provide the opportunity to find those valuable pearls from our own life experiences.

Before we continue reading *Midnight Hour* or *Darkest Hour* at the same time, I must say that my personal preference to keep the original title was profound, but in order to avoid more misunderstandings, the title was changed to *The Darkest Hour*. The title *Midnight Hour* held some sort of sacred connotation, while the new title, *The Darkest Hour*, sounded more practical.

But regardless of what you think was the best title, these hours still speak of transition periods or crises, which have the power to personally break us into pieces or break our current conditions into a new season (or a new day). And because of their relentless shifting activity, our stress levels and our personal perception can possibly elicit some unbearable attitudes and take us to a very demanding state of mind. To better relate this with another practical example, think of some turbulent waters similar to those storms of great magnitude that can swipe everything that doesn't have any solid foundation.

But even though these transition periods have great possibilities to break into new seasons, the breakthrough depends on the way we embrace our own crises and how we pay attention to all the small things that pop up during certain situations. Sadly, our own emotions, the external distractions, and other interferences tend to redirect our attention to other voices rather than helping us stay still and wait upon our Holy Spirit. We should even consider how our own emotions play a major role in these dark events and how they could be the ones we should blame the most (rather than people) because they are the ones that can take us downhill and deteriorate our true self in making our heart descend, instead of helping our true self to ascend from these episodes.

During these darkest hours, our own situations will escalate, our perception will fade away, our fears will try to take over, our hearing will become more imprecise, our emotions will appear more unstable, and a sense of direction in certain issues will seem to be less visible and more complicated. So why is it important to embrace these tragic circumstances? Why are these darkest hours so critical for our lives?

I cannot give you all the answers in one single chapter. I can only help you understand the difficult moments everyone is going through (including those dear ones who we may know). Our awareness about darkness in general terms (including our personal hours during crisis) has influenced our own faith walk and the way we behave with others (or think of others). During these personal periods of crisis, we inevitably open our hearts to so many different messages, and we become like a sponge that absorbs a lot of different information and experiences a range of feelings that take place inside our little bubble. We even become more sensitive to learn things we thought we were not ready for. But as normal human beings that we are, we incline to be more negative than positive when tragedy and misfortune knock at our door. Our normal reaction to survive these heartbreaking periods puts us right away in a defensive mode or even in a self-protective attitude, questioning all those possible ifs and should-haves while we are trying to clear all our blames and our doubts that appear during these difficult times.

Unfortunately, these difficult times become so important because the way we think during these periods will have some influence on our future decisions, and our decisions will have the power to influence our fate (destiny). It is like a muscle memory. We get so entrapped in our own crises we forget the fact that every time we foster a thought, we are developing a belief. Then without considering its normal process, the development of such beliefs will generate certain mind-sets. And without argument, our mind-sets end up shaping our own identity (our own character), and our own character will put the final lid (or closing chapter) to our purpose in this life (whether that is as a complainer, as a positive change agent, or as a person living with resentments, etc). But at the very end, we must understand that every personal purpose we gain from these darkest moments will affect the type of culture we leave behind for our next generation. This is why we have seen so many people playing the victim role from one generation to the next. It is like creating a domino effect for the next generation, and if we don't stop certain personal cycles of negative thinking, it will continue going and going and going.

Can I take this idea about our own negative inclination a little deeper but with a sense of innocence we used to have as children? Isn't it awkward how we have changed with time? When we were just little children, we didn't get scared so easily (I am making a reference when we still had pure and innocent hearts as children). It was during those early years when we would dare our little hearts to find the right place and the right time to tell (or hear) scary stories in the company of other children (or talk about certain fables that have gone from generation to generation like "La Llorona," a Hispanic tale of a crying woman who would roam around dark streets at night looking for her children). But as we have grown older, the sense of our physical and spiritual awareness has changed since we have adapted other means—as times have changed, we put our trust on other means. I would venture to say that as children, we would put our trust on God, on our invincible parents, or even on our own mental heroes; but with time, that trust changes to our own capabilities based on our own information. Thus we believe we must protect ourselves so we can be less vulnerable to the unknown, and this is because we have become more insecure and fearful about everything that is radically changing around us.

I guess the more we think or rationalize everything, the more anxious we become. Our rational thinking has made us believe we have more available options on how to approach, how to box in, how to seize, and how to control the things of God and the things we cannot see, instead of embracing the awesomeness and magnificence of the unseen things and of God with complete trust and humility. But our knowledge has made us more arrogant and insubordinate, making us believe that we must take control of everything in this life.

I think in order to understand stress, it is best to start understanding that we will face different seasons throughout our lifetime and that if we prefer to embrace each season of our life as a winter, spring, fall, or summer season to help us understand that *nothing is permanent*, we should. But even during each of those seasons, every season has its own shifting activity or intense activities, and these shifts or violent activities are the transitions that take place from night and day. And allegorically speaking, they are better known as midnight hours because they mark the change from an old day to a new day, but they, metaphorically speaking, also represent the darkness of those transition periods, which can become the most unexplainable, indescribable, and unfamiliar events in the lives of those who are going through a difficult distress.

Some of these questions we ask ourselves during our own dark hours of the soul are the following: Should my tomorrow be another day like today? What waits for me tomorrow? Can I survive another day? This dark period will always test the strengths and convictions of every person facing significant events in their lives. I am referring to a test that normally brings a struggle so strong to the where we contend with our own beliefs and place us at a daring posture, which puts all our personal abilities (physical, spiritual, and emotional) at risk during circumstances when we are not sure about what our next move should be. The best of us becomes our greatest enemy, and such self-awareness can take these opportunities to make us believe we still have the means to survive and outlive the crises to such point of aggravating the real purpose and intention of this darkest hour. I am making reference to the aggravation our own attitude may cause because negative attitudes can defeat our best outcome. Arrogance, stubbornness, pessimism, sarcasm, etc. are some of the negative attitudes that can easily be masked by faces of dignity, sovereignty, authority, etc. These "best of us" attitudes (sarcastically saying it) will direct our hearts to miss the main goal of these events because we will fall short from properly handling these crises within us or while showing support to others.

Please understand that I am not contradicting myself. We can still be strong if we are strong, but don't mask any weakness or any weak areas during the process. The transparency that you can offer to yourself is the best starting point; truly knowing yourself is wining half the battle already.

Whenever we don't learn to face our own vulnerabilities, we will expect the same from others. It is like hearing people saying to others "It is not that bad. Get over it and get back to your duties," but this type of attitude only shows that people don't know how to confront their present reality and decide to delay any dealing until future or later opportunity and many times assuming that time will always take care of things. What they don't know is that such negligent attitude of confronting their present reality is similar to signing up a blank check saying "It is not time to collect right now. I will deal with these thoughts in the future" without realizing that the future time will also charge them with very high interests from all that time that their issue was put on hold. This is the reason why transparency with ourselves is a must.

What are some of the major issues that will emerge during these darkest hours? Some people will be challenged by incredible fear and uncertainty or wrong attitudes and perceptions. Others will be challenged by unavoidable changes and unrealistic expectations. Again, we are all different, and anyone who is trying to survive any crises or life-threatening struggles by natural instinct will try to handle their own circumstances with so many different approaches—trying to resolve their issues of uncertainty, fear, doubt, negative attitudes, unrealistic expectations, and unavoidable changes. But how much of that gets truly resolved, or how much of that becomes a bigger issue in our future because we had chosen not to deal with those issues until years later? There are no easy answers, but a clear understanding of our darkest hours can only help us go through those times, make a break through that will benefit us, and help us not become another victim who got broken in two.

Chapter I

THE PRINCIPLE

Rules are not necessary, we can change them, break them,
or avoid them, but principles must be appropriated.
—Hiram

If we truly want to accept and properly welcome these events during our lifetime, we must appreciate the principle and the impressions these experiences have over our lives. The spiritual principle and the tangible impressions of each experience go hand in hand. It is just like saying pain in our body cannot be completely appreciated if we don't have an idea where that specific pain is physically located or what's causing the pain. Again, I cannot say this enough, but any midnight hour (or darkest hour), spiritually speaking, is neither day nor night. It speaks of a time and a season that is about to change, and it is a place between two periods. If the words *spiritually speaking* made you uncomfortable, please stay with me and think of them as personality speaking so you can relate. Our spirit is what makes us different from everyone else, but we will get to this in a future chapter. Unfortunately, regardless if you are a spiritual person or not, these darkest hours are never welcome because we don't like changes. Changes demand a conversion, and every conversion requires that we let go of something in order to receive something else. This transaction becomes very unwelcome and inexplicable because we don't know what we are going to lose in our let-go hand and what we are going to gain in our receiving hand.

Since we are very unique individuals and no one is exactly the same, the process involved in our personal changes (conversions) are not the same for everyone. There are conversions that have a slow process (with an unnoticeable violent activity in their mist), but there are also those conversions that can cause dramatic grief in our lives (those with violent and unstable activities).

One great analogy to these two differences can be appreciated when we think of two different persons who are diagnosed with the same type of cancer (let's use lung cancer as an example). One of them had been diagnosed with an already-advanced state of cancer and has only very few days to live, while the other person was diagnosed with the same type of cancer but with much longer time to live. The family of the second person with a longer life span is being influenced by a conversion that will take a more uniformed and slow process to cope with all the inevitable and expected adjustments. On the other hand, the first person, who received such a short notice, has more violent and shifting activities, which may cause a more dramatic grief in a short span. Sometimes we are given the opportunity to select our option between a conversion with a slow process or a conversion with a violent and unstable activity. This option becomes available to us when we keep a regular health checkup. Having regular health checkups can help us minimize those violent and unstable activities. This same principle applies with Mother Nature. Sometimes we are given plenty of opportunities to prepare ourselves for natural disasters, but sometimes, those violent and unstable activities occur in a blink of an eye. And just as regular checkups are vital to our existence, so is our proper care of Mother Nature.

To understand the variance of how our darkest hours can occur during our lifetime—whether they come with a slow process or arise from unexpected circumstances—think of them like a hurricane or a tornado that is approaching an area, and all of a sudden, the sky is getting darker. Sometimes, these drastic changes in the atmosphere can give fair warnings that things are about to go pretty ugly, but sometimes, they can also take us by surprise. The same fact can happen with our darkest hours.

While trying to present an ample and detailed manuscript about this subject, I studied everything I could learn about the midnight hour. I searched books, investigative reports from National Geographic, watched movies, listened to songs, among others. I found it very interesting that the Hebrew word for *midnight* is *khaw-tsoth* (Strong's no. 2673), and it means "the middle [of the night]." Its root word means "to split in two, to divide." The Greek word is *mesonuktion* (Strong's no. 3317), and it means "midnight [specifically as a watch]." It is a compound of *mesos* (middle, in the midst of) and *nux* (night). In more practical terms, it was as if we were being asked to pay close attention to something that was going to be split in two.

And don't we feel like getting split in two when a lot of stress or suffering is all over us? At that point, I feel like I was on something very interesting. Then I decided to select all the biblical narratives that would speak about the midnight hour. During my research, I discovered the differences between all those different biblical events and how significant these events became because of the participation from those individuals who were involved. To make things a lot easier to understand, making reference to the previous comment I made about some people making profit from our darkest nights of our souls, those biblical events demonstrate that God doesn't just say "Let there be misery on earth" or "Let there be punishment on humankind." But can I say that after God created the heavens and the earth and everything that we see in it (according to the book of Genesis), He also created laws and principles that would govern all living organisms. Using another illustration to explain my suggestion, let's take the process of a caterpillar. The caterpillar doesn't transform into a butterfly because of its seventh day of existence (as it is, the metamorphosis process varies in every case), but a butterfly comes to existence because of the process (a principle that was already established).

Where am I going with this?
We are constantly being bombarded with manifestations of many conversions, shifts, and sudden

changes. And it appears that these changes are becoming more violent each day. These changes are not the results of direct intentions from God or the unseen, but they are the results of our own participation and an inexplicable process that we, directly and indirectly, have been involved with. And as much as we want to ignore the spiritual part of our beings (or personalities), it is here when I can clearly see God's involvement with humanity.

We are still agents that can create changes or circumvent changes—not directly by the push of a button but by our conduct, our behavior, our attitudes. And although our attitudes are still being developed or changed by our own experiences, their consequences cannot be avoided.

Let's forget about God for a few minutes, and don't make this book another religious debate. But in order to appreciate this book, the readers must picture their lives like one spiral ladder. The steps we take can either take us higher or lower on the steps of that ladder; our steps are either leading us to a superior level of reality, or it can also take us down to the lowest level of deception and corruption.

But why a spiral ladder? The spiral ladder will help us see the many familiar seasons we have been dealing with throughout this journey. But these different seasons, as much as they have the potential to be very familiar to us at times (like a déjà vu experience or the four seasons of the calendar year—if you prefer to see them like that), they all present different challenges every time we walk through them. And the reason behind this speculation is that we are all connected. Whatever one single person decides to do or not to do, act or not to act, or behaves, it doesn't affect that one person only. Our actions and nonactions will always upset and alter someone else's world. Here's another great illustration how we are all connected (I enjoy giving illustrations). Let's consider a person who departs this world with a very violent activity (unexpectedly) and leaves behind more questions than answers because of suicide, a plane or car accident, or any other tragic event. If this person departed this world with a heart full of resentment or different kind of pending issues, those issues don't leave with that person. People who didn't have the opportunity to handle their differences with this person or people who still had other pending issues connected to this person, who is now deceased, will have to find a way to reconcile those differences and honor any part in their lives that wasn't honored while that person was alive. We are all connected, and honor is the bonding agent that makes connections possible.

What it may take a person to go through a transition of seasons will have an emotional impact and tangible influence in someone else too. But whatever that force may be, it can easily fluctuate with someone else, and that principle must be respected, honored, and revered, regardless if it is different from our own philosophies, viewpoints, and values.

These transitions are inevitable and unpredictable to everyone, and they don't remain in a single state (or with a single person). They have the potential to influence a whole community, family, organization, workplace, or large fellowship. As much as it may appear to be a very familiar experience to us, that same experience can be influencing others in many different ways. That's why this spiral ladder can be a little bit complex or complicated; the perception we get from this specific familiar experience can alter others' when we give our insensitive support in ways we didn't meant to.

Again, where am I going with this?

Although these periods of transition (or crises) have the potential to influence a whole community, family, workplace, etc. (or even the whole nation), it only takes one person's sensitivity to properly sense what's going on behind the curtains (with God, or hear the voice of God) and neglect to participate with God to align these shifts or extreme activities to generate peace, goodwill, and reconciliation during these darkest hours. When we participate with the unseen, it is the same as saying someone was at the right place and at the right time.

Don't get me wrong, I will always respect the views and attitudes of those people who prefer to avoid any affiliation with God. But even if I make some spiritual references, I think this book can still assist everyone to go through their darkest hours regardless of culture, education, religion, beliefs, or faith.

And as I mentioned earlier, I searched every possible document, song, and reference to make this principle about the midnight more striking and relevant to our darkest hours. With this in mind, there are also many songs I found with lyrics making reference to their own midnight experience, but I selected the following old song that perfectly describes the proper atmosphere, which can take place during any darkest hour. Even though this particular song may have a romantic background, the crises is obvious.

> Whatever it is, it'll keep till the morning
> Haven't we both got better things to do?
> Midnight blue
> Even the simple things become rough
> Haven't we had enough?
> And I think we can make it
> One more time
> If we try
> One more time for all the old times
> For all of the times you told me you need me
> Needing me now is something I could use
> Midnight blue
> Wouldn't you give your hand to a friend?
> Maybe it's not the end
> And I think we can make it
> One more time
> If we try
> One more time for all the old times
> Midnight blue
> I think we can make it
> I think we can make it
> Oh, wouldn't you give your heart to a friend?
> Think of...("Midnight Blue" by Melissa Manchester)

Back to the biblical stories that I found about the midnight hour, these are also great examples to establish the principle and appreciate the impressions this hour generates. I will explain in the next seven scenarios how the darkest hour was able to challenge different persons or incidents as these people who were involved. They were the main protagonists of these stories. These protagonists or events were transformed by the critical and radical shifts of their activities. I added some comments in a more actual setting, which can help us understand how these darkest hours are inevitable and can be very real to us not only in a biblical context but how one person's spot-on participation with this violent and shifting activity can make a huge difference when he or she is sensitive to what's going on behind the tangible tension and real pain of their own darkest hour.

> Sometimes we get the opportunity to prepare ourselves for devastating events in our lives, but sometimes we don't have such luxury. Either way, the emotional and spiritual consequences cannot be undermined. We are still delicate and precious vessels at the hands of any adversity and hardship experiences. (Hiram)

Scenario 1

The darkest hour during a social or collective tragedy.

In a More Actual Setting

This scenario, regardless of the generation, can be related to those immigrants who have gone through their darkest hours while leaving their countries to find freedom and liberty from their barren conditions, or it can also apply to those groups of people who have been discriminated by the current system.

This biblical story took place during the midnight hour (or the darkest hour), when God decided to display His sovereignty and decided to bring an unquestionable and irrefutable ending to a system that had been oppressing His people for so long. But before we understand the best part of this event, we must go and visit few verses back before this darkness took place in the lives of many people (Exodus 10:21–29).

But we cannot leave out all those movies made by Hollywood about this specific event like *The Ten Commandments* (1956). During this movie, or any other narrative related to Moses, we can see how God selected this man, Moses, to bring the Hebrew people out of bondage. But God proceeded with Egypt in a progressive approach before He allowed darkness to cover the entire land. There were ten plagues that fell on the Egyptians, but these ten plagues also affected the lives of the Hebrews.

The manifestation of the power of God during these ten plagues was not the product of an unbalanced act or disorganization from God. God's actions were purposely arranged to bring a definitive transformation to an entire community. With this said, I will continue to consider that not every disaster or personal crisis comes suddenly, but sometimes, we do have the opportunity to modify our beliefs, prepare ourselves, or have the opportunity to readjust our navigation compass. Another good example that comes to mind about having an opportunity to readjust our navigational compass is when two people cannot get along and their struggle to understand each other can become so stressful. Yet if one is taken away (without notice), the one left behind would suffer the consequences of unresolved issues because that person didn't take the opportunity to settle their disagreements before the permanent departure of the temporary opponent—who knows, perhaps after speaking about those issues, that person could have been the other person's best ally. Life cannot be taken for granted. Nothing lasts forever. Do not leave pending issues for later!

The Bible is full of allegories, parables, symbolic events, and extraordinary accounts to demonstrate the transactions God made with those people during biblical times. Nothing was taken by mere accident. There was a reason behind every word that was spoken, every illustration that was given, and every number or name that was utilized. On the original manuscript, *The Midnight Hour*, I took the time explaining all the ten plagues and the reason for their arising magnitude. But it is not necessary to spend time suggesting the meaning of each plague. Our goal is getting to the midnight hour (darkest hour) of this whole significant event.

These were the ten plagues that affected both Hebrews and Egyptians:

1. God turned water into blood.

2. Frogs covered the land and entered in the Egyptians' homes.
3. A manifestation of lice that attacked a lot of persons.
4. A plague of swarms of flies that invaded the homes of people.
5. A serious pestilence (disease) that destroyed their possessions (livestock).
6. A breakthrough of boils on people and animals throughout the land.
7. Thunder and a lot of hail that came from the heavens.
8. The appearing of locusts that consumed all vegetation.
9. Thick darkness that was overspread all over the land for three days.
10. The death of every firstborn.

The ninth plague was just the beginning of the darkest hour for the Egyptians and those Hebrews who wouldn't follow certain instructions that were given by Moses. Although this thick darkness was the most decisive part of God's divine arrangement, it had an enormous amount of distress, suffering, and pain, but it was also necessary so God could complete His objective.

After this thick darkness (still referring to plague number 9) the death of the firstborn was about to take place in Egypt. The firstborn of all men who didn't follow Moses's instructions was going to be slain at midnight. Death was to do its part now.

It is interesting that two great characters in life enjoy meeting during this time, Darkness and Death, which take tremendous pleasure, giving an spectacular showdown during the midnight hour, and that's the reason why such hour is still feared.

Then the final plague, which took place at midnight, came about without sympathy and kindness. It was the death of every firstborn at the midnight hour, in which God was also preventing the bark of every dog to be heard. Dogs are an illustration of every voice, every person, every ministry, and every influence that has been tormenting people for so long.

Please compare this similar event with the crucifixion of Jesus when He had cried out to God demanding why He had been abandoned to such point that he felt so hopeless.

Can you see the desperation and desolation? Darkness is bad, but sometimes it is necessary. Darkness can also be part of God's plan. During the crucifixion of our Lord Jesus, thick darkness was felt, but at that moment, the curtain of the temple from that religious temple that covered the Most Holy Place was torn in two, from top to bottom.

While separation and certain death have an appointed meeting, our own hearts will display where we are putting our trust during those crucial moments. Are we putting our trust on our educational status? Are we putting our complete trust on our politics? Are we putting our faithfulness on our status quo? Are we putting our complete dependence on certain family members, boyfriends, or certain leaders at our workplaces?

The main idea on this scenario was about Pharaoh's heart, which got hardened because of his own attitude against an inevitable change to his system (or structures). Although the activity of conversion was a slow process in which he had plenty of time to consider and adjust to the new, proposed changes, his strong mind-set didn't give any room to let go of what needed to be let go. This only created an outcome that was going to bring pain, suffering, and much affliction to the whole nation. This same principle applies to the trust we are so inclined to put on religion, on certain traditions, on specific political parties or leaders, on a world system, and all those patterns, personal habits, practices, or structures that we have become so depended on.

Sometimes the writing on the wall has been so obvious for us to see, and all the warning signs are announcing something needs to change, or they have always been there telling us to let go. But when we become so faith blinded to certain things or traditions or personal stubbornness, we will lose the ability to hear properly and will no longer have a good sight to pay attention to our own consciousness, and that's when we set ourselves to be influenced by our own stubbornness, emotions, and those prejudices that will make us fall deeper into the darkness of our own soul. This is a principle that applies to all of us, and stubbornness will get the best of us if we think we got everything well figured out.

If you want to read more pertaining to this paragraph, you may consider these verses: 1 Samuel 17:43, 24:14; Psalm 22:20; 2 Peter 2:22; Exodus 22:31; Isaiah 56:10–11; Matthew 7:6; Luke 16:21; Philippians 3:2; Revelation 22:15.

Scenario 2

The darkest hour during personal suffering affected by a larger cause.

In a More Actual Setting

This scenario can be related to those individuals who have been labeled as unfit or categorized as unacceptable because of those who still hold prejudices, discriminations, and injustices on others and are carried out by societies, religions, political motives, or cultural differences. This scenario can also be related to family members who go and serve in the military. While they are waging a major war away from home, no one is certain these family members will come back alive.

Let's consider another biblical story that took place, once again, during the middle of the watch (or at the midnight hour) when God decided to show His manifest presence and provide a winning strategy during war. A frightful, mighty warrior got the attention from God as he kept the watch and couldn't give himself to any sleep.

I am referring to the times when the invasion and influence of Midianites, the Amalekites, and the Arabians became so oppressive to the Israelites that their enemies made them cry out to their God for help.

It was until the Israelites cried out for that support when their God sent a prophet to them, and it was during another darkest hour that an angel appeared to a soldier named Gideon while he was threshing grain behind the winepress. Again, another emphasis was made that this whole exchange of arguments between Gideon and the angel of the Lord occurred during the midnight hour (the darkest hours of the night).

If we bring this specific event into a more practical approach, we may have a better appreciation of the whole story. Sometimes it is not until we hit rock bottom when we start asking for help. We tend to be so stubborn at times that it is until our days become so dark (pitch-dark) and cannot see an exit when we start asking for guidance. This illustration of Gideon is the best example—when a soldier finds himself cornered and doesn't know where to turn. The narrative even mentions that he was hiding (behind the winepress). Again, you are going to hear me saying this all the time: "Darkness and Death had an appointed meeting," but my desire to draw attention to darkness and death is because during this crucial and critical hour something is about to die or "let go." Darkness and Death are showing up to collect something, and if we let go of that something, they can easily leave us alone (this could be a radical mind-set, some prejudices we have been holding on to, some sort of dependency, or probably just plain ignorance). During this specific visitation, the death of a fearful worker brought the resurrection of a real, fearless warrior.

We can label Gideon as someone who was good in hiding and working timidly, one who was good in making excuses and one who was insecure about God's voice and reacted with fear during many occasions. But he was the only one with a desperate heart to face this experience—he was awake in his own way, and he was asking for help, ready to make whatever changes were necessary about himself.

It always amazes me how whatever we see on the outside of people is not always what their heart is saying—some people claim to be so strong, yet they are the most vulnerable, and at the same time, when other people appear to be so frail, yet they are the most resilient people.

But this specific event gets more interesting because here we can see a sentiment that has overwhelmed an entire community. The oppression from the enemy was so intense that everyone's heart was in one accord, believing that God was not with them anymore.

Couldn't this event be similar to natural disasters or even community tragedies (e.g. shootings happening at commercial centers, schools, or local parks)? These tragedies can emerge with such magnitude that our own minds would shift right away choosing to believe that God is not there anymore? When these beliefs are drawn from our hearts (as it was on verse 13) and from our own personal experiences, we consent an unforgettable impression to be raised to such point of sensing the shadow of death making its rounds around those circumstances and in our midst.

Pause and think for a minute, What comes to your mind first when you hear the phrase "the shadow of death"? Why does this shadow of death need to make itself present? Isn't it enough with everything else that we must deal with (anguish, isolation, loneliness, pain, distress, etc.)? I personally think we don't like to speak about the shadow of death because we may have so many pending issues that we still don't want to kill (or surrender or let go). These pending issues could be an unfinished career, an ongoing relationship, waiting for a dream to come true, etc. And hearing about the shadow of death in our midst is like telling ourselves, "I am not ready to die." And there is nothing wrong with that, but this attitude only shows our natural tendencies. We tend to think too much about our possible future and constantly forget to embrace and enjoy our present reality. We are in so much hurry trying to get to point Z from point A that we don't pay attention anymore to what point we are at that moment.

Was that Gideon's problem? Don't know, but he was able to transform or change the circumstances (or his own character) because of his own disposition.

Gideon was not the only person struggling during the midnight hour. Jacob was another individual who was very stubborn to change at the beginning. But there are still too many Jacobs out there who haven't ceased fighting with God during their darkest hours because of their own stubbornness and cunning mind that doesn't want to give up during their darkest hours.

While the duration of this transition may take few days for someone with the right attitude (humbleness and acceptance), it may be completely different and may take longer for other people who are not willing to learn something from these cruel experiences; for these people, it can take months of painful dealings (or perhaps years because time is not a respecter of persons) until death does its part.

The idea about the midnight hour has been extremely damaged by Hollywood movies, religious people, and those who cannot embrace these times as great opportunities of change. As human beings, we don't like to face changes, and very few people enjoy changes in their lifestyles. They have trouble changing eating habits, traditions, work environments, family matters, etc. because of fear and the feeling of becoming uncomfortable to new ideas or new approaches (or new attitudes), which can make them susceptible to failure, disappointment, or unhappiness.

> People who hate changes are
> the ones that have become confined
> by their own mind-sets about everything in
> life.(Hiram)

I can only encourage people to accept changes more often and take those changes as opportunities or as signs of living. Every living organism is constantly changing. The date we stop changing is the date we will stop living.

Scenario 3

The darkest hour during a personal tragedy, after the death of a beloved person.

In a More Actual Setting

This scenario can be related to those single mothers, widows, any orphans, or individuals who have lost a dear friend or family member or even their entire families.

It will be during the midnight hour (again) that our salvation will reveal God to us because of our faithfulness and the level of desire we seek to have an intimate encounter with God. Why do I say this? This was exactly what happened to Ruth.

If you haven't read the book of Ruth, let me tell you that Ruth was not part of the tribe that is mentioned throughout the whole book of Ruth. When we talk about Ruth, think of a person who didn't have a family. The story of Ruth says that she had lost everything when her husband died, and her fate became so uncertain at the mercy of her own choices.

Do you want me to make Ruth's issues even more serious and difficult? Ruth was not of the same faith as her in-laws. Ruth had to learn how to praise and worship a god she was not accustomed to. We must remember when reading this story that she didn't live at Bethlehem until her husband died, since she was a Moabite (from another tribe). Imagine a young woman (being Christian) marrying a young man (being Muslim), or vice versa.

Exactly! And some people still get upset among religions. This is a fair comparison taken from the Bible that no one dares to make. So get over it!

The death of her husband can be taken as another significant event, similar to our darkest hours, even though Ruth had some options after her husband died. Ruth could have returned to her own family (parents) and not face uncertainty, but she was determined to make a change (even if that change was still undefined).

Let's condense the story of Ruth to understand all the changes (or those darkest hours she ended up facing). But there is one thing we must consider: the bigger the transformation is, the greater the pressure and challenge will be. And again, all these experiences took place during her midnight hours.

Ruth's first decision was to move forward and not to go back to her old lifestyle, even if that choice was full of uncertainty. Ruth's second decision was to go beyond Naomi's bitterness and traditions, even if her decision would put the relationship with Naomi at high risk. Naomi was her mother-in-law, and Ruth decided to remain close to Naomi because she didn't want to neglect the mother of her late husband.

Ruth's third decision was to move forward with the decisions she was making, not allowing herself to be influenced by a double-minded posture, even if this would cost her reputation.

I don't want to sound religious, but a lot of times, what we need the most during our darkest times are those times of reflection, contemplation, mindfulness meditation, prayer, or just allocating some time to spend in solitude; these are just ways to embrace our own spirituality. If we could cultivate this hunger (or desire) to properly nourish our own spirit, that desire can cause so many great things to be revealed in the middle of our darkest hours, and that's what happened with Ruth.

Ruth didn't start her journey looking for an avenger to bring justice to her misfortunes, she didn't hang on Naomi to search for her next kinsman-redeemer. And what's more interesting is that Naomi, her mother-in-law, was the next person to inherit a wealth that belonged to her (Naomi), but she was not even aware of her own inheritance rights because she was too busy blaming herself and blaming others for her misfortune. Can you see how crucial it is to stay clearheaded when tragedies knock at our doorsteps? We could easily miss the blessings (like Naomi) because we get sidetracked with our misfortunes.

The key to our transformation has to be inside out. We start by acknowledging who we really are in this midnight hour. I am jumping ahead of the chapters, but that's okay because we need to see what Ruth did too. We are not victims of darkness (like what the movies and many ministries have portrayed about us all this time).

As I mentioned, we will learn in future chapters that it is at the midnight hour when we truly comprehend who we are. But there are so many people who'd selfishly prefer not to help those in need because their transformation would mean their loss. I have seen how some parents, leaders, or so-called friends prefer not to help people in this type of need because they would lose control over them.

Again, going back to Ruth, while everyone else was asleep, Ruth learned to embrace this precious hour, and she was able to uncover the truth for her own life.

I think the midnight hour has a lot to do with our character. We were born without prejudices, mind-sets, negative attitudes, and setbacks, but as we walk the journey of our life, we begin to collect trash that we think we are going to need for the road. We put all that trash inside a sack that we carry with us all the time, and at midnight, when no one is watching or no one is there to help us, the struggle begins. That's exactly what happened with Jacob, Gideon, and now with Ruth. It was at midnight when Ruth heard Boaz's question: "Who are you?" It was like a challenge. Remember that Ruth was not part of them, but Ruth didn't hesitate to answer, "I am Ruth, and I am your handmaid." Ruth knew who she was. There is no spiritual cloning over our lives. We should never compare ourselves to other people. Everyone is special, and for that very reason, everyone needs to be honored for who they are. But that's the beginning of our own struggles—we forget who we are, and we are more prone to think who we are by the trash we carry with us.

Ruth's answer was neither. "I am Ruth, the Moabite" or "I am just Ruth, a friend of God." Ruth had already gone through a lot, but she didn't see the need to claim any titles that she could have added because of her commitment, and her loyalty and integrity to Naomi.

Titles don't always sit well with me because so many people cling to them as a protective badge to hide their own insecurities.

On that night, by giving the right answer to Boaz, Boaz appreciated the heart of Ruth. There is more to this story, but the point is this, our transparency and knowing who we truly are will vindicate our circumstances.

And once Boaz heard the answer from Ruth, his instructions were the same instructions that we will hear in our hearts if we are sensitive to everything that is taking place during our darkest hours.

Scenario 4

The darkest hour during personal distress after losing everything or whatever was most valued to us—a career, a house, good health, finances, a good retirement, a friendship, etc.

In a More Actual Setting
This scenario can be related to those individuals who have lost what they have worked their entire life for and were never expecting that all the cards were going to turn against them.

I think many readers may already be familiar with the biblical story of Job. Job was a man who had everything (happiness, great wealth, good family), a man of great respect in his community, a man with a distinguished status quo, etc. But during his lifetime, Job ended losing everything, and if you can imagine that everything is everything, we are in serious business. It doesn't get any worse than that. This type of tragedy (or darkest hour) is related to major misfortunes.

Although Job went through the most tragic and painful circumstances, he never lost his faith in God. He lost everything he had—from possessions to friends and including family. These series of events were trials that were escalating little by little. We saw this on our first scenario involving a larger number of participants, but Job's faith in God was never compromised. He knew God well enough that nothing would come against him and the relationship he had with God.

An interesting observation about this story is that when people don't know how to respond to the crises of others, the best consolation they think of doing will be trying to find logical answers or explanations about God's dealing with humankind. It is like saying, if you don't understand what is going on, blame God for it. That's what Job's closest friends were trying to accomplish. And to make things worse, their reasoning will give in to so many accusations, and those accusations may turn into presumptions that God is in the business of punishing people for so many terrible secret sins we all commit. Even these opinions didn't change the heart of Job toward his God or about himself.

In this unique parable, we can see how things were escalating with Job. It was a fight between good and evil.

Since evil and iniquity were not able to penetrate in the heart of Job through the advice of closest friends, evil decided to use another tactic that would cause a negative response from Job. This time, Job's wife was about to become part of the game too. This was a straight-out manipulation to make Job become a more negative person about everything.

And we can appreciate this scenario in our daily lives too. Often we can spot around us those optimistic people who always have a smile, an upbeat and cheerful impression in their character, but often are attacked by those whose lives are miserable and those who hold much evil, resentment, and antipathy because they cannot experience any joy themselves. As it happened with Job, these people who are always optimistic will be put to the test by those with evil in their hearts. They want to prove how long that positive attitude will last, and if people can change that positive attitude to a negative feeling, they will exhaust all their methods to achieve their goal.

Evil people get furious when they see this kind of optimism and aura on others. Evil people don't like to celebrate the accomplishment or success of others. Evil people are always competing for attention, disregarding whether others are humiliated or dishonored. On the other hand, optimistic people are governed by an unconditional love. But if this unconditional love is not there, that optimism is just another mask people can use only when things are going well. Being a true optimist is an all-present attitude that is not restrained by external factors or circumstances.

I want to say that nothing happens by chance or accident. There are no coincidences, and there are no accidents. But the question remains, Why do bad things need to happen to good people? This is a question that I cannot find its best logical answer to. And sometimes logic can become one of our best enemies (especially for me who tends to be very analytical as a writer). Our own bad decisions can be one explanation of reaping bad things in the future. And those negative consequences don't necessarily need to surface during our lifetime, but they can pop up until future generations.

The life of Job doesn't need to apply to everyone. At this point of the story, some people can easily express their valid arguments by saying, "Hiram, you don't understand, I wasn't asked to be born with this ailment (or these inclinations)." Another valid argument would be, "Hiram, you don't understand, my son (or family) doesn't deserve having this condition."

And you are completely right, I don't understand. But instead of trying to find a logical answer, I have learned to ask myself more questions that can help me unveil the true reason of any disgruntled attitude.

My first question would be, What would you do if you or your son (or family) didn't have that condition (or ailment)? And nine out of ten people may answer something like this: "I would enjoy life," then my following question would be "Why can't you right now?"

But before you start throwing rocks at me, I am not being sarcastic—although as a writer, writers can easily become sarcastic, moody, exceptionally very inquisitive, and very creative. And that's my point, nothing should stop us from becoming more creative so we can still enjoy this life.

There is a difference between those people who know how to live this life and those who only know how to exist. I hope you don't miss my point, but in order to live this life, you only need a spirit (and that's one attribute we all have). Perhaps you want your son (or family) to live their lives according to your expectations, and that's what's frustrating you. And since we only need a body to exist, the question remains the same but with a different arrangement: "Do we want to enjoy life with our body or with our spirit?" Trying to enjoy life with our body will fade right away; enjoying life with our spirit will invigorate us.

Let's wrap it up. It was during Job's darkest hour when Job displayed his most optimistic attitude, a complete trust in God. He didn't give away any space in his heart to doubt God's unconditional love for him. And if this unconditional love is real, we can sense it on us or on those people who are genuinely positive because their optimism is not conditioned to external factors or circumstances. These people understand that anything outside their essence is temporary. These people recognize that *they are much bigger* than any system or organization, much bigger than their problems, and much bigger than any offense done to them. But that quality is their inside secret. It is the unconditional love they have for themselves (because they have experienced the unconditional love God has for them, a love that, regardless what mistakes or shortfalls we make, is much bigger than our small perception of all things). If we can capture this unconditional love—and we must have it in our hearts—we will overcome a lot of doubts and uncertainties. It is very interesting to learn that at the end of his darkest hour, Job was able to say, "I saw my salvation with my own eyes, no one had to tell me about it".

Scenario 5

A time of despair and hopelessness that can make anyone think that everything has turn against us; whenever we feel how a simple rainy day has, all of a sudden, turned into a pouring day of only bad news.

In a More Actual Setting

This scenario can be related to those times when our best is not good enough and we feel as if all the events, circumstances, and people have conspired against us.

It is at midnight when our spirit will rise from any comfort zone and correspond to the rules and principles that govern our lives. It's during our periods of great distress when we are reduced to nobody because of our incapacity to use our human resources and our need for answers, and some wisdom is truly evident to comprehend such suffering. Every personal adversity has had a special way of undoing us and unveiling our true character. It is during these times when the masks of self-assurance become difficult to maintain, and perhaps we decide to seek comfort on something more solid than our own self-assurance to something more reliable than our own arrangements and on something more truthful than our own little promises.

These personal adversities have the influence to lead us to a place of solitude, and in many of these isolated times, our own hearts take that special time to reflect on things. David was a man who constantly pursued those times alone with God.

By reading some of the psalms David wrote, we can understand the richness and depth of his time alone with God. I had to mention the life of David in these series of scenarios because the entire life of David is one of the most compelling stories in the Bible—from the beginning of his early years when God had chosen him through the words of the prophet Samuel to the end of his life.

All the lessons we have learned about David whether they were introduced from the pulpit or from any serious study of the sacred scriptures, they have taught us the kind of heart he had for God. Besides being a highly praised warrior because he feared no evil but only God, his psalms illustrated the heart of a great poet and musician too. David lived a lifestyle that has influenced the lives of many, which included the Jewish, Christian, and Islamic cultures. David is seen as king of Israel in Judaism, as an ancestor of Jesus's adoptive father, Joseph, in Christianity, and as a prophet and king of a nation in Islam.

David, like the apostle Paul, learned to endure affliction, hardship, misunderstandings, and major struggles because he always looked beyond his immediate circumstances. This attitude was very possible to them because they saw God in the midst of their immediate hardships. They learned to trade the weight of feeling unloved, being unjustly judged, and being wrongly persecuted for what they knew, which was always in total control over their own lives.

Since I am not citing or referring to any specific midnight event during the life of David, it is obvious, after reading some of his writings, that David had to endure a lot of periods of suffering and isolation. I am using the life of David as an encouragement and inspiration to help us go through our own darkest hours. But what made David so special? According to his writings, David lived a lifestyle that was fully dependent on God's provisions and God's principles.

Although David was not an expert in war tactics or people didn't see him as an experienced warrior during his early appearances, the first time David displayed his courage against the enemy was at the time when he armed himself with only a stick and five particular smooth stones. This encounter was going to be a very defining moment for Saul's army and their enemies. Saul's army was constantly being defeated by a giant, Goliath. Goliath was a bronze-armored nine-foot-tall Philistine giant, and this giant was the best weapon that kept Saul's army frightened and mentally defeated as Saul's skilled warriors were cowered for forty long days. The results of this particular incident gave David the reputation of being a brave and daring warrior, but unfortunately, other stories also give accounts of David being a cunning diplomat, as well as a talented musician, a great king, and a persecuted friend, just to name few of those claims.

But we can link most of these accounts to the root of David's faith and fame, which were formed by great periods of severe trials and uncertainty in his life. David was never concerned about entitlements (titles) or personal recognition.

In the midst of his loneliness and struggles, David opened up and shared his thoughts, struggles, fears, tough questions, and prayers through his writings. While he found himself alone in the dark, on the run, or being kept unseen through enemy's territory, David learned to be fully dependent on God. David was never a perfect man nor a perfect leader, but his years alone with God humbled him and broke him (especially at his darkest hours), which contributed to develop a heart that was totally surrendered to God. This kind of heart fostered a life that has created a legacy, which has endured from generations until this day.

The writings of David can be easily comprehended by the heart of its readers because they can connect with

David's complete trials and chaos. We can also notice how David's writings share a breakthrough during his own struggles—a breakthrough that always maintained an internal compass in David's heart, a personal heart that had always pointed to God Almighty. Whereas most of us look for external happiness or external resources during our periods of great trials, David shared the deeper joy that is grounded in a relationship he endured with God.

Why is David's life so attractive to people who are experiencing times of transition and serious breakthrough? Because David's writings teach every reader to drive their hearts toward a place of deeper well-being, a place where our heart is developed to trust God beyond our external abilities and own realities.

Psalm 119 is the longest psalm, but the Word of God is all over it. David, the author of such psalm, knew God in a very personal and intimate way. David knew that during the seasons of trial and suffering, chaos and confusion, God was still in control; these special times ultimately developed a deeper and more profound joy and a stronger bond between him and God whom he served.

Again, it is worth repeating it: David learned that the keys to his triumphs were found in making God his internal compass during his periods of suffering, pain, and misery. Because of his own attitude toward these darkest hours, those periods became major breakthroughs in his life.

Scenario 6

Personal regret or disappointment with painful guilt.

In a More Actual Setting

This scenario can be related to those times when we have come to the misunderstanding and awareness of all those times we have done so much wrong, and an unhealthy remorse is accusing us of all the bad choices we have made with our life. These times can cause a ruthless depression or can drive us to extreme misbehaviors. Because of this hopelessness, we may even feel as if suicide or other wrong doings were our only options.

Our darkest hours are the worst time we should pick to get comfortable or distracted. We are becoming so used to rapid answers and finding everything with the click of a computer mouse that we don't want to work hard for anything anymore. This concept about rapid answers is good because we cannot claim ignorance as an excuse anymore, but such concept has its downside too—not everything we see, read, or hear is real. So we must do our own work to differentiate between what is true and what is fake. That is still our responsibility. But let's keep it real. The reasons why we don't want to be diligent or attentive during these periods of transition is because we don't know what to expect next.

Things have changed so fast in the way we expect things now. Getting rapid answers or fast deliveries of the merchandise we buy have changed the way we expect things now. Rapid solutions have given us the false expectations of demanding exactly what we are expecting (to include the time it takes to get our answers and the authenticity of that product we have been expecting). But whenever we don't have a clue on what to expect, our lack of diligence and lack of attention during these periods settles in us right away. Since there is a lot of uncertainty about what comes after our crises and the fear of being very vulnerable or the anxiety of not achieving certain expectations (and the list can go on and on), our hearts and minds get distracted with other things that are more certain.

It is obvious that if pain and suffering are more certain at that moment, we cannot divert our attention to other things that appear less certain.

The list of influences that will distract our mind/ heart during our suffering are surreal. But don't get me wrong, we do need some form of distractions to help us minimize the pain, but we can make a list of good distractions and bad distractions that will be shown as we deal with our own darkest hours.

I think you got the message—I am more concerned about the bad distractions.

The bad distractions will definitely bring negative influences during our crises, and these can damage the process of the transition we are going through.

Whenever we are going through difficult times, it is expected that we try to put our attention on other things that can bring temporary numbness or detachment from our present suffering. Unfortunately, these are also opportunities to ruin other things that don't need to be ruined or other people who don't need to be neglected, as we are paying more attention to some distractions that would bring us temporary pleasure or detachment. The pursuit to gambling, addictions, extreme isolation from the rest of the world, infidelity, pornography, or other forms of immoral conduct can be part of a large list of those negative distractions that can do more harm than good to our lives and our relationships. These types of distraction can easily take place during our darkest hours because our own awareness and perception of reality gets weaker to the point, to such level that our emotions create certain confusion, rebellion, opposition, resentment, etc.

Religiously speaking, these negative distractions are labeled as sins, *hamartano*, which literally means "to miss the mark." Although these kind of distractions will keep knocking at our hearts for their attention at all times, we are more susceptible to entertain these distractions when things are not going well in our lives.

Forgive my sarcasm when I mentioned "religiously speaking," but the reason behind my sarcasm has to do with the manner in which we have been taught what sin is. We have been fed the wrong conception that actions—such as adultery, gossip, murder, stealing, lying, etc.—are the definitions of sin; and this has robbed many people from becoming better persons. Morally speaking, if people don't commit those types of sins, these people can be great saints because they don't have any problems with sins, such as adultery, murder, stealing, etc. But as persons, if these same people have attitudes of arrogance, pride, supremacy, egotism, etc., these people are still missing the mark (they are still sinning).

So why is this subject part of the darkest hours? Let's visit the Bible once again. In Matthew 6:23, we read a warning about our discernment—how it can turn bad if we don't have a good vision. And I am referring to a vision that makes us miss the mark, then our whole perception will turn dark. And if the light we think we have is actually darkness, how deep that darkness can be! Where am I going with this? It is very humanlike to accuse others for the misfortunes and accidents we face. Sometimes we do it to the point of seeking some retaliation when we get hurt and feel anger toward somebody else. We think these people need some help, but whenever we seek retaliation, we feel superior to others, or we don't honor people, we are missing the mark as ugly as committing murder, stealing, or doing pornography behind closed doors.

And to make the problem even greater, carrying extra trash in our bags is also missing the mark. Carrying that extra weight with us is not productive nor beneficial. As the Apostle Paul wrote to the Corinthians, "Get rid of every unnecessary weight (drop it!)." Again, all these are negative distractions. Don't pay attention to any distractions that don't help you with the process.

Distractions can happen very easily, and they start by being unnoticed.

The book of Mark, chapter 13, speaks of end-times (religiously speaking), but it is more about a period that is ending and a period that is pushing our circumstances because it wants to show up. Yes, I am talking again about the midnight hour, which, wrongly, has been always translated or interpreted as a sign of the end-times. But the emphasis that was made on this chapter (Mark 13) was not about the end of times, because the things that Jesus mentioned in this same chapter have happened in history already. But the highlight was about to stay alert at the times of transition and *not* to get distracted when two phases are about to overlap (night and day). Please consider each verse and count the many times Jesus was calling our attention to stay alert and vigilant during our darkest hours:

> We are asked to stay awake because during this difficult time, we can become a prey of a toxic relationship, adultery, addiction, or anything that may deceive us.

> We are urged to be on our guard because we cannot afford to believe everything we see hear or sense during our personal crises.

> We are encouraged to move higher than our own circumstances because we must see the whole picture from top of the mountain, from above our own valley.

> We are admonished to keep everything away from our thoughts because if we allow certain

negative alliances to speak to our hearts, we may not make it alive.

We are pressed not to go to our past. Whatever we did or didn't do in the past it is irrelevant already, we must fix our eyes to the present so we can be ready for tomorrow, so be alert.

Again, we are advised to never stop watching over, or caring for ourselves.

We are encouraged to seek those who truly care for us, tell them to keep praying, keep the support, this is not a *Lone Ranger* movie.

We are exhorted again, to keep our eyes open to everything that is taking place.

We are recommended not to get sidetrack or unfocused, not until it is over.

We are beseeched to remain cautious about our own *self* and everyone else, to what is going on at all times.

Scenario 7

When we have been wrongly accused or paying for a judgment we didn't deserve.

In a More Actual Setting

This scenario can be related to those times when we have been wrongly accused and publicly humiliated and embarrassed by the extreme actions or condemning words of others, slamming our character with dishonor and injustice.

The midnight hour, even if its atmosphere is very uncertain because of its own darkness, it becomes very imprecise to the human mind—that part of our human body that wants to analyze everything.

With only one more scenario to go, I have been trying to do my best on describing the atmosphere of this hour by using biblical accounts that people can relate to and personal behaviors or natural settings that can help everyone compare and comprehend this experience. But as much as I can continue adding more words, one thing is speaking about it, and it is totally a different thing going through that experience ourselves. There are no words to describe what everyone goes through, whether it is because of a broken relationship, the death of a family member or companion, the news of a terminal disease, a natural disaster, etc. Nothing can be compared to the actual experience.

But there is still one more example that can take our breath away, leaving us speechless or helpless because of the injustice that is being done. I am speaking of those people who have been wrongly accused. Some of these people have spent unwarranted time in prison, and their whole life has been torn with a huge gap in their lives. What about those people who have been defamed or slandered by their superiors or others with authority, and their careers or lives have been damaged because of the wrong perception the assessment from those who had the privilege, or benefit, to accuse them, who utilized all the weight of their leadership position to dishonor them? Some people with authority don't have the compassion it takes to lift those who are going through some difficult times, whether these people's families get destroyed, their career opportunities to advance get shattered. But severe punishment has always been an indication of abuse of leadership.

I think this abuse of leadership is more evident in Third World countries, where the trauma of severe beating goes to the extreme (whether it be emotionally, spiritually, and many times financially or physically). But needless to say, any form of abuse of leadership, regardless if this happens in a Third World country or in a very progressive nation, this abuse of leadership should be suppressed, exposed, and admonished.

The honor of every person should never be forsaken by those who call themselves leaders. This type of treatment can make anyone feel useless, hopeless, incompetent, and unable to freely move as before. These actions can cause real negative emotions that can probably make anyone feel as hostage at the mercy of those abusing their authority.

These were the same circumstances Paul had to face when he was sent to prison, yet in spite of being in prison at a very dark place and undergoing the beating of the enemy, Paul and Silas were heard praying and singing to God at midnight.

At midnight? Yes, their circumstances were so unclear, and their future was so uncertain, but that didn't stop Paul and Silas to have a positive attitude. They *realized they were much bigger than* any oppression caused by their enemies. Most of us, whenever we don't understand what is going on and are wrongly accused, we become angry, we get full of resentment, we desperately want to take revenge, and we develop a very negative attitude toward God and other people.

But the positive attitude of Paul and Silas brought a "suddenly" that shook the prison. You know the rest of the story! And amazingly, the chains were broken, and prisoners were released.

Paul and Silas knew the secret of God's presence and power—their attitude, a positive attitude that was thankful in the midst of chaos and provided a channel for God's power to operate in their circumstances. They knew God will make Himself present as He inhabits in the praises of His people. But what is praise?

Without getting religious, let's think about the act of praise in more practical terms. Genuine praise is an attitude of the heart and not an expression from the lips. How many times have we seen people "praising" at churches with loud voices and then later again see these same people cursing other people? So let's put an end to this false definition. Praise done by lip service is only a form of ovation; praise done by the heart is a lifestyle.

Can I take this a little deeper?

A person who lives with praise in his heart all the time is a person who is thankful for something. We sincerely cannot convince ourselves or our minds by repeating one hundred times per day "I praise you! I praise you!" We sincerely are not a programmable computer—at least I am not. I still enjoy having emotions, and the roller coaster of my own emotions are something that keeps me alive (and not a computerized robot).

Then how do we develop this type of lifestyle (a heart full of praises)? If we were mindful and conscious at how we were created, it wouldn't take any effort or hard work from our part to feel blessed (or to be thankful). Recognizing that we were created by the breath of God is enough for me to make me feel like a superhero (and with more powers than the Avengers). But this assessment needs to be considered with a twofold perception so we don't become so arrogant with an attitude of false supremacy. When we see ourselves the way God made us (different than the rest of the world), we should also see ourselves compared with the universe. Can you see how small and exceedingly little we are (as a small speckle) when we compare ourselves to the universe? But then again, our praises should come after we realize that *each one of us is much bigger than* the next national political election, that we are much bigger than our problems, that we are much bigger than the latest invention, and that we are much bigger than any toxic relationship, bankruptcy, bank account, or career opportunity. Do you get the point? If we comprehend praise using this explanation, we will understand why praising God gave the winning edge to those biblical characters who are described in the Bible but also rebuked others at different occasions. Again, I will modify some of these biblical accounts with a more practical explanation.

Jesus spoke about the hypocrisy of the Pharisees because they were thankful to God only from an outward show and not from the heart. Genuine gratitude for the way we have been created is a matter of humility and true love for God (from the inside out). The Father is always seeking those hearts that are thankful for the way He created us. It is like a father being proud of his children and his children being thankful to him too.

This way of life, an atmosphere that is filled with people who are thankful for who they are (much bigger than their own circumstances) repeals any attack that may come at the times of transition and breakthrough. Being thankful to God for creating us much bigger than our enemies sends the enemy running, for the enemy cannot be where the presence of God is manifested.

I could have listed all the verses that speak of our praises to God, and this explanation, as weird as it may sound, would fit in every verse.

Whenever we cannot understand the whole picture of our own circumstances and our own ability to overcome the bondage or oppression that is over us, it is time to remember, *we have been created much bigger than our present circumstances*, but the Bible would say, it is time to praise the Lord, to give thanks.

I challenge everyone to start feeling like a superhero (and to thank God for creating us with superpowers, as superheroes do) during our darkest hours, and we will experience the release of God's power in our behalf just like Paul and Silas felt when they were incarcerated (imprisoned by those who abused their leadership). But unfortunately, our human reasoning will make us question if we were truly created so special (since our hero powers are not that tangible), but it is never too late to start having this kind of attitude: "I am much bigger than (fill in the blank) ," and after a while, your positive attitude will be undeniable and undisputable, to the point that others will ask, "How do you do it?" Just let them know that you got superpowers.

All the seven biblical stories can only confirm the importance and weight the Bible places in our darkest hours. Whenever the Bible takes the length and time to explain or illustrate certain issues several times, this should be a sign that our spirits (hearts) become greatly influenced by these experiences. But these biblical illustrations won't make any sense until we can make them more practical. The following chapters will present those opportunities, the practicality and veracity of our own experiences. Now that we have learned about the significance of the midnight hour, the next eleven chapters are arranged to help us build the type of resilience that is necessary in our lives to endure those difficult and dark moments.

Chapter II

EMBRACING THE
PROCESS

*Whenever we refuse to embrace an opportunity, we lose the reward
to understand the whole essence of that person or moment.*

—Hiram

We just finished the first chapter trying to explain the principle of our darkest hours in our lives. These overwhelming events can show up at our lives with many different reasons, and sometimes we won't be able to recognize their implications and true repercussions because we sink deep in the valley of our own sorrows. Nevertheless we must learn to embrace such moments and not fight them, for our own good health. It is now time to apply such principle in practical terms and allow our own understanding to manage these experiences with layman's terms that can be applied into our own lives.

Since this experience has never been easy to anyone, let me start with another question, Why has it been so hard to take the time to embrace those significant experiences that have a truthful meaning for our lives in this present time? The answer is not that easy, or perhaps, it is hard to find true answers in our hearts because we are constantly living on the go, and we are no longer taking the time to value the small things, the genuine and real things in life. But as fascinating as our present times may appear because of all the information and knowledge we can easily find during these unprecedented times without much struggle from our part, all these facts and information we can obtain, it has become more difficult to discover the essence of everything that comes into our hands. Why is this? Because we want answers, and we want them now; we don't have any more patience to wait for the answer (nor in God to give us the answers). And as we didn't work any hard for the quick answers we got, we normally recycle that same information in the same manner we normally recycle our household trash. As weird as this may sound, we have forgotten to value the truth and the substance of everything that come to us.

People can blame the rat race (the high speed) in which we are living that we are now taking less time to truly pause and meditate on those valuable things. People can also blame the lack of expectancy and the lack of patience we are now living with. This lack of expectancy from our part doesn't give our hearts enough fuel to thrust our minds into a higher dimension of our present circumstances.

At the same time, the process of embracing doesn't last long enough because people don't expect anything good in return anymore, and at the short end, we abort the true meaning of our daily encounters or our unexpected experiences. We have forgotten that nothing appears in our lives by accident. We prefer not taking our time to appreciate every moment. The best example that comes to mind for this last explanation is a pregnant lady. We can safely say that a pregnant lady can easily embrace her pregnancy because she is forced or obliged to embrace her pregnancy, because she is expecting the birth date of her new baby. But when there is no expectancy at all, any idea to embrace something is completely aborted or denied. We deny ourselves the privilege to embrace the unknown because we don't have time for what we don't know. Expectancy is nurtured with what we can feel, hear, see, and sense during those significant moments. Expectancy is also nurtured by what we have been told or the information that what we have been given related to those significant moments.

Now going back to the pregnant mother. The same principle is true when she is not expecting a baby, or she hasn't been informed about her circumstances related to other similar people, thus she doesn't need to embrace anything.

To answer my previous question, Can I truly believe that people have lost the sense of embracing those excellent things because their perception has been distorted? Where there is a poor perception, there will be a poor embracement.

Most of our perception has been formed by the type of preaching and teaching we have heard from people behind the pulpit, from the social media, from the news, and from our own family traditions. Unfortunately, some of that type of information on "how to embrace the unknown" has been taught by the same kind of people who only want to increase their own kingdoms and denominations. These people have been trying to justify or explain the crises that come in our lives in ways their groups of followers don't stop seeking their support or don't stop joining their fellowship so they can continue being subject or hooked on their next discourse.

These are some of those ignorant comments I have heard people say when they are given the opportunity to speak during someone's else crises:

> "You shouldn't feel any compassion or sympathy. That person deserved what he is going through, its karma at its best."
> "God is punishing that person because of all the evil there is in this world."
> "This hurricane or tornado is a sign from God. He is fed up with all the evil in this place."
> "God is mad. God's vengeance is being manifested."

These may not be the words you have heard exactly, but the implication of other comments you may have heard contain the same meaning. I hope you get the idea.

I cannot ignore that whenever people think of the midnight hour, their first thoughts are everything that pertains or relates to darkness. Although such perception is half-truth, it is not the whole truth. And we cannot start embracing this critical hour until we don't change our own perception about the whole concept. Although the darkest night has been our oldest and most haunted fear, there are more positive aspects about the midnight hour than the negative ones. Before anyone starts throwing rocks to people (or at me), let's go back on time and reconsider how darkness became a terrifying matter so we can understand how our own fear toward our darkest hours has an origin on the way we have been brought up.

Since we can remember, the dark has always played a major role in our lives. Before our cities were able to place invented artificial lights in their streets, the darkness was the time when people were most afraid of. People associated the dark hours of the night with great horrifying events that happened in their past, and those unfortunate events included some accounts that later helped shape their own mind-sets. And those same mind-sets have shaped some of our history throughout the world. There are a lot of illustrations and history that can be said about any area of our lives, from a military point of view, gang-related stories, medical emergencies, etc. These illustrations can cover real combat tactics during war that only happened during the dark hours of the night. There were also some real criminal acts during dark hours and, to make things worse, some real fatal accidents that have happened during the night hours too. Now imagine all these incidents taking place when very poor lighting was provided in the cities, on the highways, or at open areas.

I sincerely think there are still places in the world that are much darker than others, and at some places, people still believe that the darker it gets, the more horrendous events may happen.

Scientists can now measure the dark density of a place by utilizing the Bortle Dark-Sky Scale. There are very few places on earth that the Bortle Dark-Sky Scale still rates as one, which is being extraordinary and amazingly super dark (or true darkness), where visibility at close feet is not even available.

But going back in history, when there was no artificial light, true darkness created an instinct for survival at many places; that same instinct that was impressed on others went from generation to generation. Although the days we are living now cannot be compared to the days when our ancestors used to experience longer dark hours, some of those experiences and stories have gone from generation to generation, and that adds more weight to the equation why some people are still terrified when we related certain issues to the dark. Let me share more observations to this argument.

1. There are still some native tribes at some parts of Africa and the Middle East Desert where you can truly appreciate true darkness; these tribes have been struggling for years with nature to stay alive. It is during those dark hours when predators (lions, leopards, pumas, wolves, and hyenas) go out in packs hunting for their food and natives still live in man-made huts that can easily be destroyed by these predators. You can say that these places still illustrate the perfect scenario of man versus beast. The danger of these places have been to such extreme that natives have learned to

overcome them, but needless to say, people who have lived these experiences have also learned to associate this dark time with the danger of being the prey and being eaten alive. This threat is not only experienced in Africa but as societies around the world have to learn to fight hand-in-hand with the wild for survival. I am speaking about the jungles in South America and India too.

2. The Bible also records many facts about the city of Jerusalem when the fear of the dark was associated with Satan (the devil). For thousands of years, Satan has been an abstract opposition of light. Since Satan rejected to live in communion with God and be under God's sovereignty, he has always been categorized as the epitome and focal point of darkness. This kind of mind-set blamed Satan for all the deaths and diseases that happened during old times or ancient history, to the point that made everyone believed Satan's most active time was during the dark hours because of the hours of obscurity and vulnerability.

3. Another fact that brought sustainable fear of the dark was during the Middle Ages in Europe. There are still cities and villages that haven't changed that much with time. True darkness in the skies is still appreciated because the shepherds and those fields have remained the same as their ancestors used to live. But there was always imminent danger in those areas from people that would kill, hurt, and steal with cold hearts from their victims during the night hours. Most of

these attacks were very brutal and violent. These killers would set up traps to attack at nighttime on the country roads and kill their victims because it was their only way to gain gold and merchandise. A lot of crimes in different societies still occur during the dark hours (consider the drug lords at Mexico and other similar countries). This normally happens because of the lack of visibility and minimum number of witness.

4. Back in the fifteenth century in the forest of Romania, there was a real character whose actions were extraordinarily violent and brutal that it opened the door for the supernatural. This character helped the minds believe more about the supernatural, and people later began to create more stories about vampires, man-wolves, and monsters. This character was Vlad the Impaler, also known as Vlad Dracula. He employed tactics of punishment that were full of evil, giving him an account to torture and kill between forty thousand to one hundred thousand Europeans. Dracula's tactics included torture, burning, and drinking the blood of his own enemies. This account became a legend and, at the same time, very superstitious because the acts of this man were so evil that people believed he was the devil himself. The story about vampires came to take a different form after his name and the legends about the supernatural became more dramatic after history made an account of his acts.

5. But the darkest time of history took place in the streets of Edinburgh when King Edward III passed a law that it was against his kingdom to have homeless people. Poor and homeless people were completely abandoned at their own fate, and their only refuge was to live underground, where it was already infested by sewer lines, sickness, rats, human waste, and highly contaminated spots. If these homeless people would be found lingering open in the public streets, they would have to face severe punishment that would be carried by local authorities in forms of public beating and public hanging.

   Although their only remedy was to hide themselves underground where their sense of direction was only the smell (again, because the underground was enormously dark), their destiny was still in jeopardy. Around 1827, a pair of infamous killers who plotted a great financial gain decided to kill these homeless people at their own refuge and sell them for medical research. These killers didn't make the lives of these poor people any easier. This kind of underground murders were justified by medical science, and the victims didn't have any rights at all. This period became the darkest time of Edinburgh.

6. The lack of visibility and the inexperience for travelers to move on the dark roads during the night was another piece of information that created fear to the dark. Although we now have

flashlights, GPS, and cell phones, the difficult terrain and true darkness at some places gave our ancestors real apprehension to navigate at night. This apprehension continued to be a cause for alarm from generations to generations that still haven't conquered the phobia of many people because the dark still presents some kind of similar concern to travelers at unfamiliar journeys or accidents that take place while being asleep.

Ancestors might have passed many stories to their next generations and every country may have had their own stories to tell about very frightening accounts that have happened during their darkest hours. Graveyards have been the best connection between these stories and different characters such as the devil himself, ghosts, etc. Our ancestors have accomplished a great stimulus of fear with these facts about being attacked at night, seeing ghosts, sensing the paranormal, and seeing the devil during the darkest hour because the night hours also have the ability to sense or hear shifting sounds easily (the wind, nature, or anything else that may move).

I am not invalidating the normal fear of the dark, but these accounts can also help us understand in a small scale why we may unconsciously fear our darkest hour and prefer not to embrace it. I am just trying to paint the whole picture and understand our normal apprehension to embrace this principle in our own lives.

After reading the same order of examples I gave above, I would like to consider the possible reasons of our own apprehension to our darkest hours.

1. We may feel inadequate or unable to embrace our darkest hour because we feel the weight of our own vulnerability during our own crises (or darkest hours).

2. After feeling vulnerable, we may think we don't have what it takes to go through our own midnight hour (our darkest hours or crises) because we are very familiar with the tactics from evil people and how they are just waiting for us to make a mistake to devour us and humiliate us.

3. We may be struggling with the midnight hour (or our own crises) because of past hurts, and some people come to mind how they have taken advantage of our helpless circumstances. We may not be able to embrace this hour because of what our ancestors have also shared with us about their past. I am speaking about comments like (1) God doesn't work in our dark circumstances and (2) if you are in the dark, it cannot be God. But we must stop following such legalistic attitude, doctrine, or formal mind-set if we truly want to be transformed or go through this crisis.

4. We may think that our present condition is at the lowest level than any person who have gone before us—a form of comparing ourselves or listening to people saying that we are there because we deserve such reward—and instead of receiving forgiveness from the Father who loves us so much, we think the devil still has the right to accuse us and show his face before we can experience complete peace or transformation.

5. Perhaps the devil is not accusing us, but we still feel that we don't deserve God's forgiveness or God's favor. But our own unforgiveness will not help us embrace our transformation either.

6. We may not be able to embrace our darkest hour (a time of transformation) because this is all new to us. We have become so worn-out to what other people have said about crisis (consider the earlier illustration of Job and his friends) that any unfamiliar explanation can make us apprehensive to such point that we don't think it is going to work for us.

It has never been easy for anyone to change a mind-set. It is much harder to discard and abandon a mind-set than to consider a new idea. I included all the possible illustration to help us understand how, throughout centuries, we have framed our own mind to think dark is bad. But if we set our minds to have a different perception about our darkest hours and always expect good things after those hours pass through, we will prepare ourselves to receive more blessings than misfortunes. I am not saying you throw a party when you have lost everything, nor am I referring for you to have fun when a dear beloved is dying of cancer. But a positive attitude in the midst of chaos can nurture the right levels of expectancy to receive a new day (a new beginning) and shorten the length of those darkest moments. Remember, night is not forever (neither is day), but because of night, we can appreciate the light when it shines up. Can I share a small secret with you? Although this idea may be opposite to embracing the light in our lives, it is still true. A lot of light is not good either. People have become blind because of too much light exposure (but unfortunately, these people cannot admit their own blindness). When I speak about too much light, I am referring to those people that think they know it all.

After we have set our goal to embrace our darkest hours, let's work on other qualities in the next chapters.

Chapter III

TAKE TIME TO LISTEN

*Don't rush into conclusions or hasty reactions, stop to
listen to the sound of your own voice, and discover your
true self, you will be amazed with what you hear.*
—Hiram

There are several factors that come to play every time we truly want to embrace an idea or a thought. Let's bring back the idea about the pregnant lady again. Whenever we want to have a strong desire to embrace an idea (or a vision), our perception and awareness need to become more sensitive to the setting we are trying to capture in order to assimilate all the information we can gather. It is like trying to get inspired with a piece of art so we can understand the artist behind his work. But this can only happen if we *truly* want to embrace such thought (or vision). Even if we have had similar experiences in the past, in order to have the strong desire to completely embrace a new vision, we need to make every setting as a brand-new experience once again.

Consider the same illustration of a mother giving birth for the second time; the whole human body becomes very sensitive, and although the event was similar when the first child was born, some of the facts become undefined and unfamiliar with the second birth.

Another great illustration and the kind of example we need for this chapter is the time we can set aside to spend more time in solitude or meditation. If we start our time of solitude with an attitude that there is nothing to receive or that we are not going to get anything out of it, our true expectations will limit our ability to receive even peace or tranquility.

It is until we position ourselves to receive something when these undefined and uncertain times can speak to us. Even if it is a very small whisper, the sense of a kiss, or a soft voice calling our names, these opportunities become clearer to us when we give ourselves the opportunity to receive from an appropriate position, a position of stillness and quietness. If we start embracing with an attitude to receive, our eyes then become more alert, the ears more sensitive, and the senses more acute. But sometimes positioning ourselves to truly listen to some words of wisdom is not an easy task when we have been the ones who have walked ourselves into our own mess. I am making reference on events in which we got involved with a toxic relationship, alcohol, porno, drugs, etc. During these times, we may be looking for words of wisdom, but if we are not ready for a change, perhaps we are only looking for an oil to numb the pain. At this point, people have become so hooked into their own mess that it is hard to see if they truly want out or if they are only looking to patch up small issues to continue in their own chaos. Again, truly listening takes more work than just relating to old experiences or hearing some emotions being voiced out. Genuine listening is having the desire to capture and embrace the whole picture as if that desire was the one thing we need the most so we can learn something from doing it.

Here is where I am going to get a little bit weird. Sound is one of our greatest tools that can be used to understand a great deal of the crisis, or the transition that is taking place. Having good hearing gives a better perception and awareness of the image (or thought) that is being seized.

Although I am putting more significance to our spiritual hearing (or insight), considering that insight as being able to see or understand something more defined, often sensed while using our intuition. But this intuition is more distinct when we have learned to pay attention to all the things that are taking place at any given time.

Again, my attention goes to our spiritual hearing, which is that inner voice that speaks from our hearts, rather than our natural sense of hearing. Another advantage that deserves its importance is to listen to people with wisdom too. A gut feeling will give us a hint or a tip when these people with wisdom come to speak to our lives.

Why is hearing important? Hearing our own problems can make us feel anxious, upset, left out, and confused, and our own emotions can get real loud sometimes—to such point that we are not hearing anything else but our own emotions. This is why it is easy for us to withdraw ourselves from circumstances or events when we cannot follow what is being heard outside ourselves because feelings of frustration or other emotions can easily invade our own hearts. Confusion and difficulties become obvious and unexplainable, but if we don't realize that we may be having an existing problem of hearing loss, it would be like watching an old movie with no sound, so a complete assessment of the whole experience is impossible.

Whether we are the ones giving support to those going through a tragedy or if we are the ones suffering from a tragedy, listening is imperative and essential. As people giving support never forget the ones suffering need to tell their own story, don't rob them of that opportunity. Don't add your own story to their narrative. Don't say things like "That happened to me too." Who gives a damn about our memories when we are not the ones suffering at that moment?

If we can be conscious of cultivating a good hearing during these critical times, we will be able to achieve two great milestones: the right perception of our crises (and not what our emotions are saying) and the right comprehension that will help us wait until everything is over. What happens when we don't have good hearing? We will not notice the activity until this intensifies. I don't want to appear rude, and I am not comparing ourselves with animals, but have you noticed when animals start looking for shelter way before we do when some storms are moving our way? That's exactly my point. Why do we need to wait until things get worse when we can develop a better acuity to read people, to understand times, and to listen to our own intuition?

Let's visit the Bible again. There was a person in the Bible who knew how to wait on God, and this person was able to recognize God in the midst of chaos or any violent activity. This person was Elijah; he knew God's voice. You can read the whole chapter to understand the importance to pay attention even to a very small or soft voice that can speak to us.

When Elijah was on the run as described in 1 Kings 19 from evil Queen Jezebel, who ordered his death, Elijah waited to hear from God. His sensitivity helped him recognize God's voice even at the places or sounds that were not familiar to Elijah.

Again, why is sound so important? Sound is so vital because we must recognize the voices we hear. There are voices that will manipulate our peace, there will be voices that will invade our integrity, and there will be all kinds of voices that will appear to be sheep, but they could be wolves dressed up as innocent as sheep. Don't forget the story of Job either, since everyone will be willing to participate when we are in the valley of our own sorrows. Some people will participate just to take gossip back with them and share it around, but others will participate with a good heart trying to bring us back on our two feet. But the mechanics of just listening do not complete the whole process of perception and comprehension. In Genesis 3:8, we see Adam and Eve enjoying the presence of God because they heard the voice of God walking in the garden in the cool of the day, but we also learn that their fall was caused by hearing another voice. Does it make a difference what we hear and how we hear it? *Yes!*

Chapter IV

SEEK ALLIANCE

The alliances you select have the power to destroy you or sustain you, that's how much power they are granted.
— Hiram

Listening well, as I illustrated that quality in the previous chapter, is very important, but forming good alliances is also important. Any alliances can help or destroy people whenever they are needed the most. A great alliance is hard to find nowadays. People have become more interested on self-promoting their own interests, and most of the friendships have become very superficial. We can notice this growing disadvantage when our social media groups are full of participants competing for the number of followers they can accumulate and the numbers of likes they can store in their profiles.

We were born to be social. As much segregation or discrimination we see on the current news, we will come to the final realization that we are all connected, we need one another (directly or indirectly). Even our worse enemies, they also cross our paths to teach us great lessons in this life so we can become better individuals. People have never been the problem. The problem is how we select and succeed in life with the people that cross our paths for a reason.

And as harsh as I am going to put it, our alliances will facilitate or hinder our ability to listen or see the different messages or significant lessons that will be sensed during our darkest hours (or even during our entire lifetime). Remember that our darkest hours are very vulnerable periods for us because these tragedies tend to trigger our temperament to the extremes.

I have a very creative imagination, so I love giving examples. Imagine yourself being wounded deep in the valley and all you can do is see hills after hills or mountains all around you, but nothing else that is beyond those mountains. So you are not aware of the splendor (if any) or the different sceneries that is on the other side of those hills. But your alliances can (if you have any)— they are not wounded, and they can still run to the top of the mountain and scan the area for you (if their vision is still faultless).

Faultless? Are you sure? There are some people whose vision has always been faultless about the future even when these people haven't been in the valley of sorrows.

And that's my point. There is power in agreement. When we form alliances, we are automatically making agreements with other people. If I were to explain this concept to little children, it would be something like this: "Picking up your friends [alliances] is a serious matter. You are picking how far you want to get with your future. If you want to be an orange but you hang around with apples, you are going to end up being an apple."

Once we agree with someone or someone agrees with us, such coalition will either destroy us or help us walk through the course of such darkest hours. I can illustrate this point with the lives of several characters we have used already (Gideon, David, Ruth, Elijah) so we can see the kind of impact their lives had because of the kind of alliance they had (with God). Now if you are familiar with the stories of the Bible, consider other stories that can provide the opposite, wrong coalitions that ended with bad results (Adam and Eve, Samson, Jonathan, and Judas).

Remember, as I mentioned a few sentences back, there are many voices in this world—voices asking for money, voices of resentment, voices full of prejudices and hatred, you got my point. They all want our complete attention, but if we pause to entertain them in our heart, we are susceptible to create an alliance. It doesn't take that much effort; all we need to do is entertain those voices in our hearts to start thinking alike, or at least start giving them our support.

Unfortunately, during our darkest hours, we don't have the complete ability to differentiate genuine alliances from superficial alliances. And superficial alliances have as much power as genuine alliances have to influence over us. It is imperative that we establish good and solid connections when we have the ability to discern their motives and their hearts. Judas (of the Bible) is the most accurate example for this illustration. While we may be experiencing a breakthrough in our life, but if the alliance we have feeds us wrong information, we may be heading for our worst circumstances and never make it to see a new day. Consider the previous example and consider who we think we can depend on to see beyond our hills while we are wounded in the valley. How many names come to mind? Don't worry, all we need is one faithful alliance.

Why am I stressing this issue so much? People against us will always disguise themselves as our best option and usually as our fast solution, too, making us feel like they are the best suggestion and that we were very fortunate having them as our best coalition on our side. But please consider everything before you come to the power of any agreements.

An alliance—whether these alliances have military, business, or athletic motivation—is an agreement of friendship between two or more parties that was formed in order to advance common goals and secure common interests. And this is scary enough for me to reevaluate what type of alliances I am creating in my own world.

Are alliances that important? We do need friends, but not the kind of superficial or virtual friends we find on social media. Even Jesus saw the importance of creating good alliance when He sent His disciples in twos.

Who is with me? This should be a question we must ask ourselves every time we are experiencing distress or going through our darkest hours (periods of transition). But we must be honest with ourselves, the question shouldn't be "Who do I want to have with me during these dark hours?" but "Who is with me?" It is an honest question that only deserves an honest answer. There is a beautiful book written by Saint John of the Cross, *The Dark Night of the Soul.* The reading of this book probably inspired me to finish this manuscript, but in his book, Saint John says, "The devil fears a soul united to God as he does God himself." Our union with God during this dark hour is imperative.

Chapter V

PREPARE FOR CHANGES

*Success is determined by preparation; opportunity is
always going to knock at our door, how we answer to those
opportunities determines our chances to succeed.*

—Hiram

Can we finally agree that these periods of transition (or breakthroughs) have something to do with changes? And if you agree with me, let me take this idea a little deeper. Can we also agree that before we go through these dark moments, God will prepare us before this takes place? Remember the story of Moses, in which I explained that everything that was taking place was being orchestrated by the wisdom of God? This is another gold nugget to understand when periods of transition are about to occur. Things don't happen just because. If we go back to our own yesterday we can see the hand of God all over those events we have experienced. In other words, without comparing our personal events with someone else's, our own events could have been worse.

God will never allow something to happen without preparing or making it known to us about what's coming. Because He knows we need this time of preparation too.

For those who are parents, this perception is parallel to how we treat our own children. Because of the love we have for them, we do not want our children to be exposed to danger without preparing them first. And the reality is not so much that we expose them to danger, but we teach them from early age what's wrong and what's right. Let me explain. Some parents carefully take the hand of their little children and expose them to the stove's fire, just close enough so they could understand what heat is (or what fire does), so they could learn to become more cautious when playing with fire. The same thing can go with firearms. We don't necessarily need to scare them with a firearm, but children need to know the implications of seeing a firearm so any reckless accident won't occur, because they never know what a firearm can do.

Although I may hear some skeptics and doubters that preparation sometimes is impossible, this is how important preparation is, and sometimes makes a huge difference.

But if God prepared Jesus for His crucifixion, how much more would God do it for us since we need Him to prepare us too? Did God prepare Jesus before His crucifixion?—this could be a question from my religious friends, and my answer would be a solid yes (I will explain this later in this same chapter). The difference is not resting on God's part to prepare us but in our own receptiveness to allow Him to speak and touch our lives before this crucial period comes.

I still think I haven't made my point clear. There have been some relationships we shouldn't have engaged ourselves into, even though these relationships taught us great lessons. We could have avoided a lot of damaged that was done to ourselves and even more so to our families. From the very beginning, we felt something was not right, but our own stubborn attitude didn't want to see the signs (or the writings on the wall), and we went on and on with these relationships. Were we wrong when we felt we should have quit those relationships? Probably not.

Although I can see these writing on the wall as a preparation of what we were getting ourselves into, these personal experiences were probably the best example I can give you to make myself clearer.

Why do I feel so strong about this idea? If we cannot discern the time of preparation before a period of transition occurs, the transition will not be successful. Let me give you another example. It is a pretty poor example because I don't believe God is testing us (as some people still have the tendency to believe). But while we were in school, before passing to the next level (or class), the teacher would give us a test, right? Did our teacher prepare us students before those exams were given? Exactly! God doesn't have the need to test us, but life works in so many weird ways that it prepares us to advance to the next level in our journey.

Preparation happens very quietly and, a lot of times, without our active participation. Preparation includes bringing people to our lives who will help us go through these events. Preparation also includes bringing people who will help us learn lesson during these tragic events closer. There is a beautiful statement that says, "The teacher will only appear when the student is ready." Think about that one for a while.

Can you think of a captain of a ship getting ready to sail on deep waters but didn't prepare its crew members before they'd embark? What a devastation! Properly discerning life's preparation is the key to survive the storm (or breakthrough). God knows exactly the kind of preparation each one of us need.

There was a personal preparation that happened in the life of Jesus too. This event happened on Mount Tabor (known as the Mount of Transfiguration), as James, Peter, and John (the prototype of faith, hope, and love) were the witnesses of His transfiguration. This event took place in the midway of His ministry.

I am using biblical verses again because during my younger years, I spent a lot of time reading the Bible. I was so fascinated with the hermeneutics, numerology, symbolism, books that were not included in the Bible, and parables the Bible uses to teach us great lessons in life. But since I revisited my old notes in the Bible while writing this book, I can still appreciate the small details of this great event. When Jesus (the teacher) went on top of this mountain, the three students He took with him fell asleep (for whatever reasons—tiredness, weather, weakness, etc.) because God the Father had to touch the life of Jesus and the whole setting with no obstacles. Imagine if Peter would have been awake while the preparation was taking place, he would be asking so many questions to Jesus that he would have spoiled the whole show. Again, this example shows how God allows things to happen so preparation takes place. Once the preparation started, the experience was becoming more visible to the hearts of those who were ready. This experience was a visible display of God's glory, the appearance of Moses and Elijah who did not have a normal burial or death, these two biblical leaders of previous generations were going to influence the life of the Son of Man, the Son of God.

Why were these two lives very important? The life of Moses ended in a funeral that was carried into the Promise Land and the life of Elijah was a translated life that didn't see death. Can you imagine all those words of comfort Moses might have given to Jesus during those moments? Can you even conceive the idea of Moses sharing the pattern of the Tabernacle just as an illustration of Jesus's own blueprint of His sacrifice and humankind's destiny? Can you envision Elijah's energy, Elijah's power and strength being released into the life of Jesus? Can you see this kind of impartation taking place in the humanity of Jesus? This mysterious experience enabled Jesus to endure more rejections by men, but after such occurrence, He also experienced more sorrows and much grief. Isaiah tells us that no men esteemed him and that He was afflicted by the hands of men.

So if preparation is imperative, how do we prepare ourselves for these darkest hours? I know that getting too biblical can get tedious or uninteresting to some readers, but my point is still relevant. No one goes to the furnace, no one goes to combat, no butterfly becomes a butterfly overnight, and no rain is produced with the snap of the fingers. Everything in life goes through a preparation. We may see it, or we may not see it. But if we look for the signs, the signs have always been there. If you still are skeptical about this suggestion, ask yourself, Does a divorce happen overnight? Does a breakup happen all of a sudden? Does any bankruptcy occur overnight (and these are events that can take any person to their darkest hour)?

Chapter VI

KNOW YOURSELF

A coward is unable to love himself and love others. Love is a very violent action, and only the brave take love as their prerogative.

—Hiram

If you think preparation, listening, and alliance are necessary to properly embrace our periods of transition, we are not even close to the whole picture yet. Our hearts and minds need to take another ride to understand this whole experience.

We have learned over the years how complicated and amazing our mind works. The mind is always in constant communication with the whole body, which in return, controls the rest of the body. Our different body's reactions are only the aftermath of whatever signals our brains have sent to the body; even the different emotions we can experience during any given circumstance create different heart rhythms that can lead to disordered patterns or healthy patterns. Again, it is all about perception. Take stress or any other negative emotion as examples (e.g. anger, worry, anxiety, fear, etc). Whenever people perceive threat with the perception that they have no control over it, stress or any other negative emotion becomes evident. The same can be said about the times when we feel relaxed, accepted, appreciated, loved, and grateful. These good emotions are sent to our mind, and the mind then process the messages to the heart. Then the mind responds, accordingly at an increased state of calmness, and our heart's coherence will stop any obstruction to be in agreement with the mind, then such state improves any person's ability to make decisions, heightens mental clarity, and increases creativity.

On a side note, I also started a manuscript months back, *Conspiracies of the Mind* because I was amazed of all the manipulations our mind does to us. I studied college courses about the mind trying to decode the reasons why we behave or misbehave the way we do sometimes, but this study was not about our personal conduct with others but how we conduct ourselves with our own self.

Emotions give color and a beautiful meaning to our lives, and for better or for worse, these same emotions influence many of our decisions and actions. They come and go, faster than the speed of thought, showing up in our brain activity before we even have time to think about them.

I cannot emphasize this enough, but we normally evaluate everything as we perceive it and think about it afterward (if we go back and think about it).

Our Lord Jesus made a very clear statement about our hearts. Our hearts are like a warehouse or supply room. The kind of provision we have, whether it is good or bad, depends in the kind of hearts we have.

To understand the importance of perception and the role that our hearts play, we must recognize what *perception* is. According to psychology, philosophy, and cognitive science, *perception* is "the process of attaining awareness or understanding of any information that is presented." It is the process of receiving and collecting data before the action of taking possession or comprehension of a matter by using our senses, mind, and experiences.

Perception is one of the oldest fields in psychology that has great physical stimuli, but unfortunately, its extraordinary effects have been greatly ignored by most people. What people perceive is the result of interplays between past experiences, sources of information, personal culture, and the self-interpretation people give on what they have become aware of. According to psychology, two types of consciousness are considerable regarding perception: phenomenal consciousness (any occurrence that is observable and physical) and psychological consciousness.

Phenomenal consciousness is, in most cases, what people utilize to reach logical solutions by simply applying their human sensation. This familiar process is also known as passive perception, which takes place according to the following sequence of events: surrounding → input (senses) → processing (brain) → output (reaction). On the other extreme, the theory of active perception emerged from many extensive researches pertaining to sensory illusions. This theory of active perception can be figured out as a dynamic relationship between description (in the brain)　senses surrounding, all of which hold true to the linear concept of experience.

Active perception is the psychological consciousness that is formed while we pay attention wholeheartedly to information we believe is already validated and truthful and have no desire to question the source. The amazing process of perception regularly changes what humans see. When people observe "something new which becomes of interest" with a *preconceived* idea about it, they tend to take those ideas (impressions) and see them (or include them) in what "something interestingly new" has taken place, whether or not they are there.

This problem has always existed from the fact that humans are unable to understand new information without the inherent bias of previous knowledge. A person's knowledge creates his or her reality as much as the truth, because the human mind can only reflect on those things that it has been already exposed to. When objects or troubles are viewed without understanding, the mind will try to reach for something that it already recognizes in order to process what it is viewing—that which most closely relates to the unfamiliar from our past experiences makes up what we see when we look at things that we don't comprehend.

What's more interesting to me is that the mechanics of impregnating a new idea or a new understanding using sound and visual effects while preaching behind the pulpit recognizes the need to stimulate the senses and brain activity so the person's sense of reality can be driven to such point to accept the new understanding as truth. People behind the pulpit realized the enormous influence these effects would make to the person's perception that some of them even opted to become more interactive during their preaching. Once a person accepts a new idea, a new concept, or a new understanding as truth, such reality becomes part of his or her process to analyze those events that can be unfamiliar. Unfortunately, preconceptions can influence how the world is perceived, and these can easily set boundaries to our awareness on the whole picture that is taking place. In other words, our world can be easily manipulated to be accepted if it is given with stimulus. What was unfamiliar to us can easily become familiar even if we haven't seen it. It all depends if we, or people, can manipulate our own perception. If I were to say where the high point of this book is, this is it! This is the most important part of this book. Right perception has never been so critical as it is now. Our own heart will show us where we stand during our darkest hours. We are either going to be afraid, we will be able to be still, or we may run with our emotions like a roller coaster. Don't forget, from the very beginning, our minds have been the ones to feed our hearts, but eventually, the responsibility is still on our court.

Our heart is either going to display an unconditional trust that God is in control during a time that is very unfamiliar and chaotic to us, or it is going to display a preconception based on previous experiences, voices from other people, external factors, false religions, and man-made ideas, skills trying to help us stand the storm. During these dark times, we are only going to withdraw from our own warehouse or supply room. Our own perception about the midnight hour is already in our hearts. What comes forth is just the display of it. Our only question is, Do we know what kind of supply we have to endure the storm (darkest hour)?

Chapter VII

Don't Lose
Your Vision

*Expectations are a complicated gambling game, but the
absence of vision is an everlasting forfeiture.*

—Hiram

Our darkest hours are not regular events in our lives.
These night-to-day transitions are not an everyday
occurrence. These shifts are not what we normally see
happening every day with our time hours. I am making
this distinction because we all know some people who
like to use the victim card, and that's not what these
experiences are. These difficult times are turning points
in our lives that bring a huge pause in our lives and
force us to stop everything we are doing to reflect on
whatever brought us to such point. If embracing an
idea or a thought started with the perception of such,
perception is also important to keep the right vision of
our lives as well.

Countless times, the vision we have about ourselves
also gets fuzzy and unclear. We may begin seeing in
ourselves a person that we want to hate, dishonor,
condemn, or even feel so miserable for. We need to be
honest and ask ourselves what we see. We cannot let

those thoughts linger in our minds because those same thoughts will later form the wrong awareness about our true self. These darkest hours are going to give us a double vision, yesterday we want to hold on to a single vision we used to have previous to these events. The suggestions form people; our own emotions and current circumstances will cause a negative influence over our vision. That's why we must be prepared to have an alternative at hand (e.g. friends or family with wisdom who can help us to maintain a good vision of ourselves).

Vision is as important as listening because whenever people cannot see beyond their circumstances, they can easily be deceived and be thrown from wave to wave, from doctrine to doctrine, and from one suggestion to another different belief. Since our vision is related to our eyes, it is safe to say that our eyes are also part of our spiritual perception. Jesus told us that our eyes are the lamp of the body; they symbolize and reflect the inner strength that empowers the person. The eyes are seen as the revelator of the soul's content.

Let's pause for few minutes and consider the eyes of a person who is standing guard inside its foxhole (a *foxhole* is "a hole in the ground used by troops as a shelter against enemy fire or as a firing point"). The eyes of that person standing guard are critical to the whole company of combatants. He/she cannot close his or her eyes or go to sleep, lest the enemy will take over in a blink of an eye (yes, that's right, that fast!). If we lose sight of who we are during these hours, we will allow things, circumstances, people, and previous experiences to take us to a more dangerous trips, extreme guilty trips, or a short journey to make us feel so ashamed and humiliated. I am talking about all kind of trips that can easily destroy our honor and the integrity of our true self. We don't need anyone— no friend, no family member, nor ourselves—to destroy our honor during these darkest hours. What we truly need are people who can help us preserve our own honor during these difficult times. Even if the person going through these miserable experiences were the cause of the darkest hours, destroying their honor can only make things worse.

At the present speed we are moving, the term *watchman* (or being a guard) is not just for special people anymore. Paul exhorted everyone to stay with their eyes open at all times. That's why he said that we must remain watchful and on our guard at all times; that's why he exhorted us to have a prayerful life so we can remain sensitive at all times; that's why he advised us to stay awake and alert and vigilant, attentive in all things, and he also exhorted us to remain diligent on our obedience.

A good vision of ourselves can guide us and enlighten us whenever everything appears to be dark, uncertain, and unfamiliar, but poor vision can also accomplish the opposite. It will take us to the wrong path, and it can make us feel unworthy, undeserving, and not good enough for others. Again, this perception (eyesight) is not given overnight but developed with time. If we want to develop good eyesight, think about Paul's exhortation that was mentioned earlier and reconsider the ministry of a watchman and apply that same concept to our own benefit. Any person standing guard must remain faithful to self. Their integrity is a must to clearly communicate from his point of view all or whatever that is seen coming. As watchman (or standing guard), we must be true in our message and say what we see as we see it—we must deal with it in that present moment, and if we need to ask for help, don't hesitate to ask for help. This attitude can give us the seriousness to communicate exactly what we sense, see, or perceive (with no variables) so we can deal with those feelings immediately.

There is a lot more that can be studied about the biblical ministry of a watchman, but the meaning of these few scriptures in our personal study can help us see the importance of the watchman's eyesight. Vision is important during our times of darkness.

Chapter VIII

THE STRUGGLE IS NOT EASY

The real struggle in any war or conflict is not on what you don't know,
it is on what you have achieved and what you are not ready to lose.

—Hiram

Think of the midnight hour as one of those times when it seems like numerous conflicts arise to their climax at once. Why numerous conflicts? It all depends how much garbage we have been carrying with us until this point. If we have been dealing with pending issues and we have been carrying a heavy bag with us, the struggle will intensify. If that would be the case, the urgency to debate different arguments will appear at this time, and such arguments will be inevitable. If we have been holding unto some resentment, those faces are going to pop out from our memory lane. If we have been holding unto some fears, those fears are going to pop out of our own closet.

But this intense struggle has no interest in finding the middle ground. Death and Darkness will challenge our position and arrogantly will say, "Show me all you got!" Then one of the contenders is either going to die or remain at his present condition at the end of the conflict.

But someone is going to learn to let go of something. But if the person doesn't learn to let go that which he or she has obsessively cherished so bad, he or she will let go an opportunity to empty the sack of trash or let go of the opportunity to see a new day or let our own life go during this struggle. That's why it is called the dark night of our soul, and the struggle won't be easy.

The midnight hour is always about the most critical struggle during our lives, and a particular question is always going to pop out during these opportunities. The question may not be said exactly with these words, but the same anticipation from our part will challenge the moment of what we are about to face—"Are we up for it?"

Using another biblical character, we will see how this single question reappeared in someone's life several times. Abraham's life is the best example of those several times when he had to ask himself that specific question, Am I ready for this? Am I up for this?

If we want to take the side of the other contender, between Abraham and his life events, it is like every time Abraham went through his life events, life would be asking Abraham, "Show me all you got!"

If we are not familiar with the life of Abraham, it is necessary to say he faced a lot of challenges that deserved to be considered as his darkest hours too. Abraham made seven critical decisions during his lifetime, and these decisions made him learn to walk by faith. Abraham wasn't born with such great faith, it is not like he was coming from a lineage of high priests and kings, but every decision Abraham did (every separation he made) brought a significant revelation of the purpose God had in life. Little did Abraham know that God was preparing (as a previous chapter explained), or developing, his heart in which God could entrust all His secrets and promises to an earthly vessel. Abraham, just like all of us, was also accompanied by friends and family who would bring wrong counsel to him, and such wrong suggestions only produced tragic consequences. But regardless of all the obstacles, God continued to work in the life of Abraham because His Word is always true and eternal. Abraham experienced specific and critical circumstances that after going through those difficult times, he was able to enjoy the effects of his own dedication and persistent obedience. Again the principles of cause and effect are not exclusive to only certain people.

Those difficult times or persistent obedience occurred when

1. Abraham separated himself from his own kindred,
2. Abraham separated himself from Egypt,
3. Abraham separated himself from Lot,
4. Abraham separated himself from his wife, Sarai,
5. Abraham separated himself from Hagar and Ishmael,
6. Abraham separated himself from Sodom, and
7. Abraham separated himself from the promise God had made to him, a son of the promise.

I could write about each separation with detailed information, trying to uncover the emotional distress and grief that all types of separations cause to our hearts and sometimes minds too (when financial afflictions are at play). But just imagine when people have separated themselves (1) from their own family, traditions, and friendly atmosphere because of job relocations (overseas) or (2) from places that have provided all the means to supply for their needs, whether this was a stable job or a country with great medical and financial opportunities. What about separating (3) from family members who, one way or another, had been there for them, regardless of their flaws or our own flaws or (4) from their own spouses, who, after so many years of being together, they just couldn't work a problem together with, and if they did, that solution made the problem even bigger because of their own stubbornness.

Although these experiences are coming from a biblical story, the application remains the same. What about separating ourselves from (5) those people who have brought negative influence to our lives? Can we let go of them? Although we have been bonded to them because of all those intimate moments we have shared together, do we need to remain together if this connection has been a very toxic relationship? As you can see, the struggle is not easy. We have built our lifestyles around these circumstances and people; letting things go is not easy. What about separating ourselves from (6) a political system or a social environment that used to have great values and good standards, but after a while, we only see more corruption, perversion, and lack of integrity in the leadership being displayed? Are we going to close our eyes just because they are part of our own favorite political organization or social plan? Oh god, I think this one truly hurts someone. And as a final suggestion, (7) what happens when people separate from those affairs that have been the most cherished and treasured matters that have occupied their hearts— the promised son or only daughter, the career of their dreams, the fulfillment of a dream, etc.?

Are we up for it?

Our darkest hours may have something to do with some sort of separation (let go), and they are not easy at all. Again, I would do an injustice to Abraham, trying to describe all the emotions and thoughts that he must have felt during each of these separations. But the picture we can see for ourselves is very clear. We cannot compare ourselves or others when they are facing their darkest moments. Their struggle is not easy. The understanding they need is part of the required help that must be present.

Chapter IX

REMAIN FRIENDLY

It is very easy to be friends with the familiar, but it takes true character to remain loyal in the brutal test of new friendships.
—Hiram

We are always making connections at those different places we spend most of our time—whether these are at the local supermarket, doctor's visits, school, etc. Our intentions to connect are meaningful because we are very social people. It is part of our natural being. These connections could also be normal whenever we go through difficult times (it is a could-be, not "necessarily are," because we all handle these difficult times in many different ways).

But this chapter is not about forming more alliance anymore. I am speaking about a single bond between two personas. And let me explain this suggestion with our own private and intimate way to look for that special person we all have. Whenever we find ourselves in a difficult situation, whether it is a car accident, a hospital run, unexpected financial problem, etc., our mind will automatically bring the name of that specific person whom we can rely on or depend on (a father figure, mother, husband, wife, brother, sister, best friend, etc.).

This thoughtful connection varies with everyone because such connection is related to the person who is always there in our hearts whenever we need him/her. Again, to some people, this strong connection may be a parent, a spouse, a true friend, or a relative.

Our Lord Jesus became aware of John's heart because John intentionally made Jesus his vital connection. And I think this is where I am taking this idea: Who is your vital connection? It could be your spouse, a friend, a mother, a daughter, etc. Once you find your vital connection, the next question will be, Does your vital connection has his/her most interest in you? Are you a priority to his/her vital connection too?

We can discern John's heart by carefully examining some scriptures that speak about John (the disciple whom Jesus loved) and learn about the bond he made with his teacher, Jesus. The following fourteen examples will bring a better idea about John's special connection with Jesus.

1. Throughout the scriptures, James, Peter, and John seemed to be the most intimate students of Jesus, because they accompanied Jesus on several special occasions; one of those occasions was when they followed Jesus to the garden of Gethsemane.

2. Because of their favored relationship with Jesus, James and John also sought special position in what they mistakably assumed to be Jesus's earthly kingdom.

3. James, Peter, and John were the only ones permitted to follow Jesus when Jesus raised the daughter of Jairus.

4. John was the only disciple who was with Jesus Christ from the beginning of His ministry, during His crucifixion, and as a witness to His resurrection.

5. John was the only disciple who decided not to run away or hide from authorities when the times of persecution and conviction from the Roman authorities were at their highest point and when the Jewish Pharisees and Sadducees were rumbling toward them.

6. John demonstrated loyalty and faithfulness to our Lord Jesus, and at the same time, he was greatly loved by Him.

7. When Jesus sent messengers to enter into a village of the Samaritans to make that place ready for Him, the Samaritans did not receive Jesus and His disciples; John and James saw this and asked Jesus if they should command fire to come down from heaven and consume them like Elijah did.

8. Jesus also sent John and Peter to go to prepare the Passover. They were to enter into the city and meet a man carrying a pitcher of water, who would show them the house where they were to prepare the Passover for Jesus and His disciples.

9. One of the greatest accounts of this relationship that John had with Jesus was when Jesus committed His mother to "the disciple He loved," John, while our Lord Jesus was on the cross.

10. The Gospel of John can also give us a great picture of John's heart toward our Lord Jesus. John's writings are considered the simplest yet

most profound content of the four gospels. It seemed as if John put a lot of emphasis on those most critical and most difficult times that our Lord Jesus lived during His earthly ministry. He moved beyond the obvious facts of Jesus's life to a deeper and more reflective meanings; these are truths about Christ and how we may know God in a more personal way.

11. John was able to communicate a vision with a heart that was completely devoted to his mentor. John was able to impart a message that neither the Greek philosophers nor the Jewish teachers conceived. "The Word became flesh and dwelt among His people."

12. The Gospel of John stands by itself, if compared to the other gospels. The other gospels have so much in common that they are easy to compare side by side, but John's gospel is the only gospel that doesn't clearly identify its writer—perhaps as an act of humility.

13. The love of John toward his teacher was so profound that he embraced every word, every action, and every thought that was coming from His teachings. This consumed heart was committed to enter into the heart of his teacher, and his teacher knew that too; in return, His teacher helped John to develop a heart that would be completely surrendered to Him. John got to the point of completely abandoning himself to the teachings of our Lord Jesus; he sought his messiah for every event, every question, and

every circumstance. This was and is still the real meaning of being a disciple.

14. Jesus became everything to John, and because of such attitude, Jesus did not withhold anything from him.

In closing, who is our real friend whom we can completely trust with our life to? Who is our vital connection that can provide vitality to us when we are being drained? Who is the true source when we need help, immediate comfort, and will never leave us nor forsake us? Can we truly be like John and seek him/her on all our dealings, questions, problems, issues, and concerns? There is nothing wrong if your answer is God or Jesus, but neither is wrong if you have another person whom you can have a strong bond with too.

Chapter X

WHAT PURPOSE DO CRISES HAVE IN OUR LIVES?

Many persons have the wrong idea of what constitutes true character. True character can only be formed in the fire, but it is tested by how we treat others: with honor, nobleness, and greatness. Anything lesser than that can only come from a mediocre, average, and second-rate creature.
—Hiram

The midnight hour is inevitable. If we want to experience new beginnings, we must go through the crucifixion of our own past hurts, failures, defeats, and even man-made accomplishments. The midnight hour is a critical and unavoidable event for nations, churches, and humankind. We cannot experience a new day unless we leave behind our last day. A new day can only come after or from a dark night (or from the dark night of our soul). We cannot go to the other side unless we venture to cross the ocean of our own uncertainties. We must live with the purpose to grow, and every growth requires a change. And every change requires a sacrifice, and every sacrifice demands a death. This is a principle that none can get away from.

Our own lives are marked by this principle from the very moment we take our first step. Perhaps we were never told that our faith, our life process, our journey, regardless of our beliefs and traditions, consist of constant changes, phases of surrender (letting go), dependency, and death. Just like the same parable of the seed that was explained by Jesus when He compared Himself in that parable. It is only when we give our self a certain death and truly die to certain attachments can we truly experience real life. But as unfortunately as I am going to say it, we must experience many deaths too, not just one.

When we were children, we didn't have much to worry about. But as we grew up, our minds and hearts began to treasure so many things we were told. With this, prejudices began to bottle up inside our hearts. Fears, arguments, misbeliefs, mind-sets, prejudices, and misunderstandings were just becoming part of the huge list of things that we have been carrying in our bags during all our lives.

There is an old song that can give us a clear idea about this life process:

> When I was young, it seemed that life was so wonderful
> A miracle, oh it was beautiful, magical
> And all the birds in the trees, well they'd be singing so happily
> Oh joyfully, playfully watching me
> But then they send me away to teach me how to be sensible
> Logical, oh responsible, practical

And they showed me a world where I could
be so dependable
Oh clinical, oh intellectual, cynical
There are times when all the world's asleep
The questions run too deep
For such a simple man
Won't you please, please tell me what we've
learned
I know it sounds absurd
Please tell me who I am
I said, watch what you say or they'll be calling
you a radical
Liberal, oh fanatical, criminal
Won't you sign up your name, we'd like to
feel you're Acceptable
Respectable, oh... ("The Logical Song" by
Supertramp)

After all we have been taught and all the tactics, strategies we have developed to survive, or all the scams and tricks we have learned to become more undependable (perhaps we have become more dependable), there comes a time when we realize we must surrender all the bad stuff we have been gathering—all the bad stuff that has made us think so wrong about others or about ourselves or even that stuff that we may think is good stuff because it makes us feel more superior than others.

Although this is the shortest chapter of the book, I cannot speak of what needs to be surrendered (or *let go*) during our darkest hours. This could well be a toxic relationship, a codependency on someone, the fear of feeling unaccepted, the apprehension of a bad choice we made, and the list of many different things can be as large as this book.

This period of breakthrough is very personal to each one of us. In this period, we are either going to break our self or break through something. But the preparation to go through these difficult times has already taken us this far, and there is no turning back. The death of a family member or a faithful companion can also be part of the preparation stage to finally let go of something we have been carrying in our trash bag for so long.

It is the principle of life from death, and it is when we apprehend the idea that something must die in us so we can fully live. If I can say it like this, because of all the trash we have been taught (or we have been learning ourselves) throughout the years, there is a time we must bring the death or our man-made self so we can release our true self. Self must be put to death because the more our "self" surrenders, the greater is our real freedom and true spiritual growth. Now as we are almost in the last chapters of this book, what is so special about our spiritual growth? It is our spirit that gives us life and the only true source of energy to live.

Chapter XI

TRANSFORMATION IS UNDENIABLE

Personal transformation cannot be hidden; it has global effects. Our only solution to save ourselves from killing each other is a personal revolution to end what must end in each one of us.
—Hiram

As we are coming near to the end of this book, we are appreciating more the principles and the right impressions behind the midnight hour. But please don't get stuck on principles, and get ready to break all the rules because God is much bigger than principles and because our own life is much bigger than rules. The midnight hour is all about a transformation that is taking place, and God is involved in such events because every life is important to God and every life was uniquely created by God. But after bringing so many characters from the Bible to this study, there is one character who is always mentioned (yes, always!) when it comes to transformation. So how could I have forgotten about the life of Jacob? I didn't; I was waiting for this chapter so he can be the best example here.

If people want to illustrate a major transformation, we cannot ignore Jacob's experience with the angel.

And just like Jacob had an appointed time for a divine transformation, we will also have our own appointed times during our personal journey. The Bible doesn't hide anything from us. If we seriously search the scriptures, we will find secrets after secrets, shortcomings of people whom God used powerfully, and many accounts of human weakness and obstacles that didn't want to participate together with God on behalf of all humanity.

This chapter is not about Jacob's deceitful personality but about the night he wrestled with the angel. Interestingly enough, God gave Jacob a special dream before this struggle took place. Speaking of preparation again, right?

What a wonderful god, right? He shares His plans with us, He prepares us, and He sends the help we need during our darkest hours. There is a promise in the Bible that says that God will never leave us hanging.

This specific dream might not have been a day or few days before the struggle, but God's words will come to pass. The ladder that Jacob saw in his dream can have many different applications, but they all relate to a progressive ascension, an ascending-and-descending interchange of a close relationship between heaven and earth. To this day, there has been an increase on the awareness of our spiritual reality. There are now many doctrines and weird practices trying to construct such ladder, and on the other extreme, there are also those trying to avoid a ladder because of fear, religion, and mind-sets.

God, in His infinite wisdom and endless love, allowed Jacob to pass through some very painful trials—trials that were, little by little, shaping the main event of his life. That day came when God appeared to Jacob once again and asked Jacob to go back to his native land but promising him that he was not going to be left alone.

If you read the scripture, did you notice God's comforting and reassuring words "And I will be with you!"? Thus, Jacob obeyed God and moved both himself and his family out. And as Jacob and his family were on the way to Canaan, God appeared to Jacob in a very special way. Read Genesis 32:24–30, and you will understand one of the most amazing moments a person goes through during his own dark night of the soul.

Can you capture this whole event? We see God dealing with Jacob even before this dark hour began to take place. God knew the right time for Jacob's hour of transformation. God caused every circumstance for Jacob to be left alone. It is only when we are left alone with God (in the dark of our own soul) when we can recognize that a change must take place, that a wrestling match is about to take place, and that we must let go of something we are dearly holding on to if we want to see a new day.

On that night, God gave Jacob a new name, a new character, a new destiny, and that is Israel. *Jacob* means "one who deceives," but *Israel* means "one who reigns with God." One thing that we should appreciate even more is how the love of God toward us has an unmeasurable amount or capacity toward us and goes beyond our own reasoning. He is more committed to our destiny than we are. He is just requiring one thing from us: that we can completely put our whole trust in Him and that we stop trusting our own previous experiences. He will make a new thing in which we cannot depend on our soul, on our education, or our own strength (mental, physical, or spiritual roots). This kind of attitude is best illustrated on Matthew 5:3. That's why a humble heart can receive much more than a heart full of arrogance. God opposes the proud but gives grace to the humble during the darkest hours.

Chapter XII

DON'T NEGLECT YOUR OWN SPIRIT

Whatever we do with our spirit is our own choice, we can neglect it, we can nourish it, or we can empower it, but we cannot kill it, for it is the breath of God that gave us life.

—Hiram

Whenever some people think of devotion, right away they think it is only a religious activity, so they shut down and prefer not to consider or reflect on that word.

But the act of devoting ourselves can have many different meanings throughout the world. They can range from daily prayers, daily Bible readings, and regular periods of fasting, to extreme cultural events such as Holy Week and the Road to Calvary traditions that exist at certain countries. But devotion doesn't necessarily need to be a religious pursuit. It can just be perceived as a normal endeavor that emerges straight from the heart and not from the emotions (or the mechanics of religion) to learn more about our spirit and how to nourish our spirit in the same way athletic people care about their bodies. If we take devotion with this in mind, it would become as a sweet aroma that has no desire to seek self-pleasure nor requires any recognition. This kind of devotion—which comes naturally, effortlessly, sincerely, openly, and genuinely without pretending what is not—is still necessary to fortify our spirit. Our spirit also needs ALC (affection, love, and care).

The story of Daniel is a great lesson that can illustrate the kind of self-care we need to give to our spirit. I am reluctant to use the word *devotion* because our perception could automatically change to a more religious duty, and that's not what this chapter is all about. But this kind of commitment releases a sweet aroma in the midst of any tribulation. It is like putting money on the bank, and once we need to withdraw money from those savings, we will have plenty of gain to use during our darkest hours. It is because this kind of devotion is not manufactured overnight, but it is best displayed during the most needed times. A lifestyle of self-care for our spiritual life is the key to endure any type of crucible.

Daniel was a man of commitment, his own lifestyle shows that he knew how to take care of his spiritual life. He turned to God for every question, and his heart sought God at all times. Daniel's unwavering heart and faithful commitment to the Lord gave him favor in the king's eyes.

Daniel's heart was full of courage. He always refused to do wrong, despite being threatened. Daniel's unwavering heart should be a pattern to everyone who is afraid to stand firm and stick out from being very different from the crowd.

Most of the times, our own heart, where the spirit resides, will guide us to the truth we need to hear, but it becomes very difficult to discern the message because we cannot be different from the majority. Peer pressure is real, so don't play the "I didn't know that" card with me. If you want to be promoted or you want to influence the lives of others to gain self-recognition, political agendas become the most popular games at any work environment or social groups. But the general idea about "the majority rules" didn't keep Daniel from staying committed to the Lord. And just as Daniel had many opportunities to please the crowd and walk away from his destiny, our journey will face the same predicaments.

Our journey will present many different challenges and many opportunities; these opportunities will either give us the options to take the easy way out from growing spiritually or options for us to continue with our own spiritual development. It is like the classic children's board game Snakes and Ladders, or Chutes and Ladders. This game was originated in India as a game on morality called *Vaikuntapaali* or *Paramapada Sopanam* (the ladder of salvation). This game can represent the snakes as an attractive lure that promotes a way to slide (diminish) with the existing problems, and the ladder as another alternative that provides more attempts to advance upward.

Obviously, when seeing the whole board, people will tend to choose the ladder so we can make it to the top and win. Unfortunately, the decisions we make are like that board game. The actual board game is played with dices, but our actual life game is played with decisions.

A lifestyle that is committed to care for our spirit (and its dwelling place—our heart) will pay great dividends when it comes to draw wisdom from within to make the right choices.

During the days of Daniel, King Nebuchadnezzar presented a kingdom that can be similar to any actual regime, any hostile work environment, or any depressed society. The king was not an easy master to serve nor to please, and Daniel was the only one who, at one time, obtained special favor from the king because of the revelation God gave to Daniel about the king's dream.

The greatest lessons on Daniel's life are not about all the prophecies he was able to declare or the dreams he was able to interpret but about the heart that stood fast and knew how to operate in the spirit at all times. Daniel's faithfulness to seek God for wisdom and guidance gave God the opportunity to bless him and spare his pain.

There are many good lessons we can learn for our times of transitions from Daniel's devotion, even during his personal periods of darkness.

Daniel was never motivated to his private devotion so others could see him and recognized him as a good man. He even had no expectations that the king would recognize the greatness of God since the king was very repulsive by putting all his advisors to death because they could not perform to this king's expectations. Daniel's exceptional trust in God gave him the ability to exhibit great power with his ability to understand dreams.

A devotional lifestyle is nothing more than an intimate relationship with God, who is also spirit. A relationship may be different from one believer to another, but intimacy is the key part of such relationship that God wants to have with us. He longs for us to bring our cares to Him and ask for His comfort. He wishes to interact in our lives, but He will not force Himself on us. We don't need to be perfectly good or blameless in order to care for our spirit. We can take care of our spiritual life just by setting few minutes each day to meditate, reflect on what our spirit wants to say to us. It is like going to the gym. The more we do it, the easier it becomes, and the easier it becomes, the more frequent we can listen to his warnings, his advices, and his instructions.

Do we need to stop drinking before we start this beneficial practice? I can answer this question with another question—do we need to get dress if we are hungry? Getting dress will not satisfy your hunger (or appetite). You may need to get dress if you want to get somewhere and get food, but it all depends what kind of food you are looking for. The nourishment for our spirit is maintained in different levels. We got those people who can fast for days, and we got others who cannot fast at all, but they give themselves to people in extraordinary ways. Either way, these nourishments and spiritual devotions are very private and intimate. I am not concerned about how people are doing it, but I am only concerned that we should not neglect our own spirit.

If Daniel's personal devotion was able to change one nation, how much more can that same kind of devotion do to our personal struggles?

Chapter XIII

BREAKTHROUGH IS AT HAND

There are no rules! New inventions are discovered when rules get broken, new art is realized when rules are broken, new technology is revealed when rules are broken, get my point? Your new you will be noticed when you break-through the rules you have placed on yourself.
—Hiram

We have come to the end of this interesting subject—how to handle our own crises and how to help people who are going through crises. People will ask themselves too many questions during their darkest hours. This book was not intended to create formulas, patterns, blueprints, or recipes that can help us maneuver our difficult times or answer all the questions. Again, difficult times are unique, and they are accepted differently by each one of us.

And in order to manage our darkest hours appropriately, we must know ourselves pretty freakin' well. When I suggest that we must know ourselves pretty freakin' well, we must understand all our emotions, accept them, embrace them, and know how to appease them.

There is another biblical story about a person going through a lot of stress. He was King Saul, the predecessor of King David. There is a story in the Bible that speaks about King Saul being in distress, and the only way he could calm his emotions was by the music little David would play to him (the same David who later would become his contender for reelections as a king, sarcastically saying). My point is about music. Music was the only thing that could calm his emotions. Although the strong point I am making is about what music does to our emotions, knowing ourselves pretty freakin' well can help us choose the kind of music that can help us invert the instability of our own emotions. Music has a lot of magic in it. Music is another chapter of the manuscript I mentioned earlier, *Conspiracies of the Mind*.

Sometimes, it would take only one person or just one incident to cause major changes. Incredible! But can a single person shift the world opposite to what the majority is producing? Can one rebellious individual revolutionize an entire community? Martin Luther King Jr. did. Mahatma Gandhi did. Nelson Mandela did. Bill Gates did. Adolf Hitler did. Albert Einstein did. Karl Marx did. Charles Darwin did. William Shakespeare did. Christopher Columbus did. And did they encounter any challenges, any opposition, and any adversity? And how long did it take for these people to overcome their own obstacles until they were able to see the light of their new day?

With an unbelievable endurance to stay on track, Noah was also another biblical character, a single rebellious person (just like the list above), who was able to change the world with an attitude that totally depended on him alone. And even when most people of his time would have thought he was weird, insane, and out of his mind, he was acting and working according to his spirit, even if it would cost his own reputation and put him in isolation. Sometimes we must consider that the success of our own darkest hours should be more important, then who cares about what people think. Our own breakthrough will be finalized once we care less about our own status quo and leave everything on God's hands.

This lesson is not about the ark but about the heart that was yield to his spirit or insight (which at that point didn't make any common sense at all). As Noah never stopped trusting the One who laid out the blueprints, so our attitude should be. God's specific instructions are always going to be tailored to each one of us from a personal perspective that is orchestrated to a much bigger blueprint. Why do I say this? I cannot highlight these comments enough: Let's not measure our potential with our surroundings, and never compare ourselves with our peers. God will unveil the blueprint of our destiny as we let go of our fears and get a grip of His Spirit.

Everyone believed Noah was out of his mind, and everyone but Noah didn't know how to trust God. Noah obeyed everything God commanded him to do. There was very little argument, or none at all, but months after months, Noah was committed to work together with God.

But without getting too hooked on the symbolism part of this story, let's consider few important nuggets about the ark of Noah. It was built of gopher wood. *Gopher* is the actual Hebrew word that once translated in early English would mean as "untranslated" ("unfamiliar," if we can use it to better explain this chapter). But if we can use some of these symbols as a hint to help us understand the process of our darkest hours, we can appreciate some similarities. With this said, the answers during our darkest hours can be found on unfamiliar places. If the answers could be too easy to find, we wouldn't learn any great lessons from these periods of distress, neither would they be too difficult to bear.

Another wonderful aspect about Noah's ark is the word itself (*ark*), which is written as *tebah*. It is used twenty-eight times in the Old Testament. In its original form, it means "something that is hidden and uncommon and not to be perceived as a common streamlined vessel." My point is that Noah built a huge ark, which he had very little control over and completely depended on what his spirit was sensing. Our times of breakthrough must be appreciated with such discernment, too, depending on the Spirit of God to guide us.

The ark was three-stories high and was coated inside and out with pitch. The Hebrew word for *pitch* is *obscure*. Obscure! Again, an obscure setting to pass into another period. The size of the ark was obviously not a job task that would only take few months.

What's my final point?

Noah didn't have a complete picture of the whole process. Noah only paid attention to his spirit to work together with God. Noah didn't trust his current acquaintances, own resources, traditions, and political or social interests. Noah just learned to trust in God and surrender (let go) whatever he needed to let go.

I sincerely believe that Noah was able to see his own breakthrough before this even was possible to contemplate or imagine. That's what made him appear so crazy in everyone else's mind. Sometimes we need to be out of our own minds to allow our spirit to guide us during the most difficult times.

Final Inquires

After my personal attempt on explaining the principle, the settings, and the impressions of the darkest hours, we can move into a healthier appreciation of this concept and understand why they are sometimes necessary as part of our own self-development.

This chapter is going to present a different challenge because we probably never took the time to contemplate our own attitudes after we went through our own painful experiences. We were just so glad and happy that those horrible experiences were finally over. It is not hard to see the personal changes we made after those darkest hours, but it is also not easy to notice them. It is like our own facial semblance—we cannot notice how fast we are changing because we see ourselves on the mirror in a daily basis, but when we come across a person we haven't seen for a while, that person will either tell us we have changed a lot or that we haven't changed much at all. But people who have gone through difficult times don't come back the same. If you know of a person who went through their darkest hour, reflect on that person before and after, and you will notice the difference. Sadly, the negative everlasting effect after the darkest hour can also apply to some people. The negative effect happens only when the people struggling during these darkest hours were able to survive because of the "best of them." If their arrogance gave them the strength to survive, their own arrogance will be magnified. If acting as a victim gave them the strength to survive, their own sense of feeling being a victim will increase.

For those people who are transparent and collaborate with their darkest hours (the darkest night of their own souls), these hard-hitting times are like fire—it incinerates everything that has to be destroyed within and breaks new ground for something better in people. And let's be honest, after some time that has gone by, those people who have been through tough times can also feel and sense to be different than the majority of people. I think that's why the common cliché "There can be no great testimony without a great test" is reasonably and eloquently well said. But at the same time, I also see it necessary to reinforce the idea that God is not in the business to be testing us at all times. These darkest hours are not tests from God. If he is God, he must know everything so that idea wouldn't make any common sense at all. What is true is that painful experiences like a divorce, a death in the family, any type of loss, terminal diseases, etc., laid enough weight on our shoulders that we finish testing ourselves with confidence how much weight we can bear. It is also true that these painful experiences can teach us who are with us or who are against us. But these personal and painful experiences are never presented to examine other people, but for the only benefit to examine our own self.

Now going back to the interesting viewpoint about how these painful experiences may expose those persons who have gone through and who haven't gone through difficult times, it would be very inspiring to name some qualities that can provide some encouragement to our own lives as we continue going through our darkest hours during our lifetime. These inspiring qualities are presented below, without setting any type of models or prejudices, because we can never forget that difficult times will affect everyone very differently. Providing a suggestion of great qualities after going through the darkest hours is taken from the fact that all military personnel, regardless of branch of service, are also able to know with clear distinction who has served in combat and who hasn't. Military people use a different language when they speak among themselves. They can tolerate sarcasm, they can become very disrespectful among other service members, and they can joke in such ways that outsiders may think a sure and ugly fight is about to break, but as a huge family that they are (regardless of military branch), they know they can rely on their brothers and sisters to have their backs at all times. With this in mind, let's use that same analogy to identify who has been on the fire and what the fire has done to the character of. Perhaps we may be able to identify ourselves with some of these great qualities.

New Kind of People

People who had spent time on their darkest hours and experienced walls of separation and division are the people who want to stand against any discrimination. They are people with no prejudices. They don't categorize people, nor do they differentiate anyone. They treat everyone the same, regardless of culture, religion, beliefs, education, status quo, or sexual preference. People who have gone through very tough times have an unconditional love to show affection to everyone, and because of this kind of affection, the word *preference* doesn't exist. They do understand that we have different kinds of people—some people who perhaps don't think like them or unable to perform as they do, but they know how to honor everyone the same way.

Are they more spiritual than others? Not necessarily. Are they more understanding and appreciative than others? These people have a different perception than the majority; they honor life regardless of differences and realize that we are all connected. We are all humans born in different places but not any different from the rest of humanity. These special people understand that there shouldn't be any walls of prejudices, biases, predispositions, racial discriminations, or other forms of injustice that separates people.

People Who Are Able to Listen

With the constant rush we are living our lives at this present times, always in a hurry, there is no more time available to stop and listen to people. We prefer to say "Send me a text," so we can avoid trapping ourselves in a very prolonged and exhaustive conversation. And let's be real, there are some people who will drain all our energy with their problems (problems that could easily be resolved by making one single decision—whether it is to terminate a toxic relationship or to stop avoiding certain places, food, or people; the required action is as simple as flipping the light switch, that easy, but not easy for people that suffer from codependency). These people don't drain others with a conscious and premeditated effort.

But on the other hand, we are so needed of people who are able to listen, people who can appreciate the here-and-now experience and know how to embrace every present moment. They don't live in a hurry anymore; they have a continuous and active listening to what people have to say (or what God has to say). Because of their great ability to hear, they are very perceptive and sensitive to others. These kind of people probably know what we were going to say even before we were about to open our mouths. They are mindful persons. They have good judgment on the things they must say and the things that cannot be said. Because of this quality, we can say they are thoughtful people who know how to be considerate and attentive to others.

People Persons

Unity means a lot to these people. They have a spirit (or a passion) that tries to unite people. Their endeavor for a union goes beyond any organization, a system, or any other affiliation. They are conscious that we are all connected and that no one shows up at our lives by accident or coincidence. These people are always welcome because of their very unique spirit that can get along with everyone without causing any discrimination to others who may have different ideas, culture, different religion, status quo, etc. These people are always cheerful, and their joy is contagious because they can find delight even in the smallest things of life.

They honor relationships because it is all about people. People are their priority, so transparency, openness, and a sense of being accountable at all times are some of the stronger qualities of these people. They possess a childlike heart (trustworthy and uncomplicated). Don't get me wrong, they are not childish on their decisions—they just don't play those pretend games other people play. Because of their constant caring for people, they can relate to the vulnerability of others. The unconditional support and encouragement these people persons offer to others is extraordinary.

People with a Song in Their Hearts

Using everyday words, I would say these people are happy people. These people are always content, grateful, and appreciative just for the fact that they are alive. These people know the difference between living and merely existing. They are happy not as a make-believe attitude that is presented to others but as a genuine state of mind. These people are sincerely thankful for the experiences they learned from others and with others and are ready to share those opportunities with a positive attitude to others, as they know how to give themselves to others. These people celebrate life by giving life. They have "dancing feet" because they have embraced their own experiences as part of life. These people have the enthusiasm and gusto well pronounced in their hearts. Their optimism and confidence can easily be envied by others because misery is not on their vocabulary. So many miserable people don't know how to have what these people already possess. These people have no attachments to time, place, people, or tangible things. Their contentment leans on the fact that the less restrictions they have (or things that can control them), the more freedom they can experience and feel. These people are all about freedom—free to be their own selves, free to express themselves, and free to learn from their own mistakes without feeling condemned or using the victim card.

People with Unselfish Motives

We all need to have a good amount of self-love so we can give love to others. No one can give what they don't have. But these kinds of people take service to the next level. It is like Mother Teresa–type of people, ready to give away their coat during winter so others don't need to suffer any cold. Unselfishness has become a rare commodity on these days because we all put our own guard before we give ourselves to people, and most of the time, we inquire within if it's worth it or "what's in it for me" kind of speculation before giving ourselves to people. But people with unselfish motives have a very different motivation. They do it because they believe in others. They probably suffered great loss during their darkest hours that everyone is now part of them. They have a strong sense of community, recognizing that everyone is part of their community (even the ones that are just temporarily passing by) and that in that community, everyone has equal rights—a community that cannot accept any forms of abuse (mentally, emotionally, and physically or even financially), and that's why their unselfish motives are very pronounced.

People with Great Insight

To think that some people have superpowers is not wrong at all. There are people who can read our hearts. These same people have some sort of sensitivity that allows them to see pictures or faces of people and give an exact description of how those people are in their hearts (assessing if they are deceitful, honest, demanding, quiet, conflictive, etc.). These people have a strong capacity for intuition; they are very spiritual people who can easily be disturbed by unnatural activities that most people cannot understand. Their inclination is prone to appreciate more the eternal than the temporal (they value more the character, spirit, courage of people than emotions, excitements, and short-term sentiments). These people are not afraid to experience the uncertainty of unfamiliar places; they like to live at the edge of the extremes to learn something new and pass that knowledge to others. These people are like adventurers who seek high-risk opportunities. The best description I can give is this: they have settled the argument between living or existing, so they enjoy life to the fullest at the present time, not living in the memories of their past nor in their dreams of their future. These people don't get stuck in maintaining a good balance; they override such impossible task with harmony or synchronizing everything at once so they don't miss a beat or minimize someone else's potential.

People Who Love Justice

Their quest to righteousness, integrity, and great values is the constant beat of their hearts. These people are moved by anything that provides the support of life. They are ministers of life. Any act of injustice that has the potential to destroy life becomes the provoking element for these people to become enemies of that act. There is a bumper sticker that says "A US Marine can be your best friend or your worst enemy." That's probably the best description for these kind of people. They despise injustice being done to people. They don't like to see people suffering. These people tasted suffering long enough that they don't need to see that on other people. They become relentless and ruthless, without regarding their own life, when justice needs to be served. They probably realized that after having survived their darkest hours and death having smiled at them during the darkest night of their souls that death is no longer their enemy, but the enemies are those who don't know how to respect the lives of others. They are against any form of manipulation, emotional abuse, excessive control, restraint, oppression, prejudices, inequity, and discrimination. Give this people the opportunity to lead, and skeletons from every personal closet would start appearing everywhere. Don't get me wrong. We all have done some type of injustice at one point; the problem is when some people have stepped on the lives of others to achieve their objectives. That's when injustice is at its more corrupted level.

People Who Are Not Afraid

Playing daredevil is not for the faint at heart. The person must have some sort of inclination to be wild and out of control to enjoy doing dangerous things. These people don't mind going to the extreme of danger or darkness to save the precious life of someone else. These people are not afraid to be labeled as prostitutes because they were seen speaking to prostitutes or as thugs because they were seen hanging out with thugs. Criticism and reproach are the least of their worries. These people are driven with ideals that cannot be measured by status quo. The status quo is as superficial as the next plastic surgery for some people who want to cover their true age. What truly means a lot to these people is reaching out to those that have been abandoned, ignored, neglected, or overlooked by a system, a political plot, a dysfunctional family, or simply by those dark hours that left these innocent people without a family, without guidance, and without any support. Their courage to invest on people is not founded on going against a system, a religion, or an organization. They have a different type of courage that is rare to see on our present days. They are not afraid to invest on people. They can do overgenerous actions for needed people or risk a lot for those in need but will not hesitate to put a smile on their faces, even if at the end of the task, the same people they helped were ungrateful, unappreciative, or ungraciously speaking negative about them.

People Who Sacrifice

When we think of people who have had a sacrificial life, the names that pop out are Mother Teresa and Mahatma Gandhi. These two persons found delight doing what they did. If we were to ask them if they sacrificed anything while doing what they did, their answer would be a strong no. They were people who sacrificed and surrendered a lot for the pleasure to achieve a dream. Jesus took pleasure of being sacrificed for us because His dream was to complete that assignment from God. That's why one of His last words were "It is finished" (or the same as "I was able to complete what I came here for"). So in practical terms, sacrifice is not what we normally consider as sacrifice. Think about these people who sacrificed their lives, what is the most accurate analogy when we think of those same people who made a sacrifice?

But before we think of the best possible answer, we need to understand that the original meaning of this word *sacrifice* was not about "something that must be given up." It is actually *sacra facere*, "with the intention to perform a sacred rite" or "to make holy." So in putting this word in its right perspective, it is something that is given to God to make holy. Now with that in mind, can we give something that is already holy to make holy again? That would defeat the purpose, wouldn't it? And knowing that whenever we refer to God, we mean something sacred, pure, clean, and worthy. With this said, people who sacrifice enjoy turning the bad attitudes and actions of people—insults, resentment, slander, hatred, gossip, revenge, envy, injustice, etc.— into opportunities for God to make them pure clean and sacred (approved by God).

How do these people do that without being too religious? It is with gratitude and with appreciation to others. That's the kind of sacrifice God wants. Being thankful to God for having the opportunity of being among those who need God and present their circumstances to God in prayer is the beginning of a *sacra facere*. That simple! We don't need to make any public announcements about our prayer life or break the Bible on their forehead trying to get their demons out, and if that's what we would normally do, then reconsider that our own demons are the ones that need to be driven out. These people live a very quiet life. They don't need public announcements about their spirituality. They don't even need our participation or acknowledgment to care for us. They just do it. They begin by making themselves present, then after prayers, they will respond to those needs they will sense during their prayer life.

People Who Are Game Changers

Do you know of any people who go against the major current? These people are courageous, and they are not intimidated by the majority. These people, if needed to be, can act as the Lone Ranger because they truly believe with an unreserved passion on the cause they are fighting for, and sooner or later, Tonto will be joining them too. These people always have a vision that can scare those who are not ready for changes. The flexibility these people have can also be intimidating. They can be labeled as transgressors, lawbreakers, rule-breakers, system-breakers, disrupters—I guess you got the right idea. But we are not talking about people desiring to be game changers just for changing those things they are bored with, no. These people are after traditions that are obsolete and outdated, systems that are not working any more, and hostile work environments that are detrimental to people or toxic relationships that are destroying the lives of people and walls that are diving us as a human race. For these people, sugarcoating the problem is useless, and it is pathetic. Existing problems need solutions, and breaking the law, breaking the rules, or crossing the line in order to change the existing problem could be the necessary means to finish with that problem. As a military service member said, "Freedom is not free," or peace is not the same as appeasement. These people have the courage to believe in changes that need to happen and will happen one way or another and cannot retreat to their own private cocoon thinking they are incapable of becoming change agents. That's the mentality of a game changer.

People Who Are Very Generous

There is a strong sense of gratitude in these people. These people are not stingy. They learned the value of giving and the principle (or law) that it shall be given back to you. And it is not necessarily because they are wealthy people; it is the attitude of giving just because they constantly realize how blessed they are. They give as being thankful for the service of others, they give because they see a need, and they give because it is in their hearts to give themselves. Whatever they have at that time—if it is peace, money, food, shelter, love, rest, hope—they just give without asking for any reimbursement from those people they give to.

Being generous has been totally misunderstood. The false impression about being generous and putting others before ourselves is not the right definition for being generous—that's being sacrificial. These people give because of their noble hearts, and they are high-minded people who value people as much as they value themselves, nothing more nothing less. Giving is just the normal attitude of their heart without feeling compelled to give because others did before them. Again, we will never be able to give what we don't have, so we *must* always have that which we want to give. If we give just because it is an obligation or civil duty, we will become miserable and despicable, which later will catch up to us and we won't be able to hide it.

People with an Unexplainable Peace

People who have tremendous sense of assurance in them supply a positive energy to others. When these people are not around, they are tremendously missed. I am not making reference to people being the center of the attention. These people don't seek the center of everyone's attention, but the core of their heart is to bring all the differences together. There is an unshakable peace in them that makes everyone else feel so comfortable and relaxed at their presence. They display harmony all over their faces. They don't try to represent *balance* or *stability* because such terms are only about robbing someone of their full value. These are firm, strong, and very determined people, but they don't need to force anything on anyone. They don't intimidate people; they attract people. Their conversation is magnetic, with a tone of voice that is not timid nor belligerent. The trust we can have on this people is extraordinary because they will not get themselves involve on things (gossip, slander, or insults) that would cause any disorder to linger in their minds. The peace these people share comes from knowing the right value of who they are. Their ears are not a trash can, their mouths are not a drainage pipe, and their hearts are not a garbage disposal. They care for their complete well-being—spiritual, emotional, physical, and mental.

These few qualities of persons who have gone through the fire are not all the extraordinary qualities that are found on remarkable people who experienced their darkest night of their souls. But at least, these qualities can give an appreciation beyond these darkest hours. An appreciation that a new day (or a new person in us) is on the making and that after everything is over, another extraordinary quality will take the stage on this unfavorable environment, which needs to see more extraordinary and exceptional persons standing in the midst of us.

The Summary

It was a very interesting study about the midnight hour (biblically speaking)—or the darkest hours (practically speaking), or the dark night of our soul (rhetorically speaking)—but while exploring everything I could possibly get my hands on about this topic, I found different charts that outlined the cycle of grief. All these charts have something in common—they generally consist of five stages:

1. Denial   This cannot be happening to me!
2. Anger   Why is this happening to me?
3. Bargaining   What can I do to stop this?
4. Depression   What's the point of me going through all this?
5. Acceptance   I think it's going to be all right!

Although they offered some good information about this issue, I couldn't completely agree with these charts because all of us are very unique in the way we handle our own grief. Needless to say, the misery over our lives can also come to our personal lives in many different ways. It can be developed by some injustice being done to us, so in that case, we may start feeling anger instead of denial. Or it can unexpectedly happen because of a huge hurricane in which depression will strike in our hearts right away after seeing all our losses, without giving room for denial (although denial can still come out later).

But as I stated earlier in this book, our own darkest hours are unique to all of us. Information can only be helpful to understand the process, but we don't have to abide by the popular trends. So don't be afraid to break the rules and go against those major trends saying that it has to be a certain way or that we have to act in a certain way. Even the information I have provided in this book falls short from truly giving you a comprehensive and more complete portrait; it can only offer you some guidance when you need it the most, or it can only help open up your eyes so you can understand the needs of others or your own needs when our world has become so insensitive so we don't harshly criticize or judge those in time of great desperation.

In summary, I just want to leave the reader with my last thoughts or personal suggestions so we can all contribute, in one way or another, whenever we see someone suffering or feeling hopeless. No one needs to reach the point of suicide, and no one has the right to drive people to their misery. Most of our darkest hours are provoked or even amplified because we didn't feel we were being honored. Honor means a lot to people, and when we don't take the time to honor people, regardless of our position of influence or authority, we are depreciating them or devaluing their worth, whether it is at home, at our workplace, with our friends, etc.

There is a saying that there are only two things that are guaranteed and definite—our taxes and death—and everything else is temporary and disputable. Although this common and popular saying is reasonable and very appropriate, I would like to challenge the reader with a third element that will challenge that popular perception. The third element that is also guaranteed to happen while we are alive is change. Changes are inevitable. Changes are part of every living organism, and changes are irreversible. On the precise day we are born, we become susceptible and predisposed to suffer changes throughout our entire lifetime. These changes will create some uncertainty. Other changes will be forced on us, and they will cause certain pain or suffering. And other changes will help us foster much gratification or contentment in life. Changes are not only necessary but also part of our own development; whether we decide to cooperate with these changes or not, they will demand our attention or, at least, makes us aware that our lives have been influenced by them.

Unfortunately, the volume of this book was based on those changes that are being forced on us. And those violent changes (alterations or shifts) during our lifetime, which perhaps we may not see as being forced on us because of our negligence or lack of participation, are still part of the process that is called life. We don't mature by age, but by the damages we go through—or to use a more straightforward phrase "by our own experiences." And most of our experiences that help us mature include some measurement of pain, suffering, discomfort, agony, and the list can go on and on.

That's why it is to our benefit to become familiar with the cycle of our own grief after learning who we really are or what aspects of life trigger our negative emotions, what brings peace to our relentless behavior, or how we analyze and manage our own experiences. If we know ourselves pretty well, the grief cycle won't be that ugly.

The next aspects of the grief cycle can help us remember our own dark night of our soul, but it can also help us understand those people who are asking for our support while they are facing their own grief.

These are the aspects of life that may get triggered during the Denial phase of the grief cycle:

1. The person may enter in shock and mistrust.
2. The person can also feel confused and experience panic.

These are the aspects of life that may get triggered during the Anger phase:

1. Blame God, blame others, and blame self for the circumstances
2. Hostile toward others or self
3. Have many direct questions of why and how

There are the aspects of life that may get triggered during the Bargaining phase:

1. If I could start …
2. If only God could …
3. If I were not … *or* I were a …
4. If I could have done…
5. If …

These are the aspects of life that may get triggered during the Depression phase:

1. No longer interested in usual activities or everyday chores.
2. Loss of perspective—no longer having a desire to consider or to engage.
3. Everything becomes a struggle, even the simplest things.
4. Seeks isolation or do the extreme of being overly involved in the lives of others.

These are the aspects of life that may get triggered during the Acceptance phase:

1. A fair acceptance of the circumstances
2. A reasonable amount of acceptance of any losses
3. Willingness to try options
4. Becomes more inclined to let go
5. Begins to adapt and stops fighting

It is necessary to add two other phases that are not included in most of the charts that speak of the grief cycle.

The Readjustment phase (in which the person reconditions the mind to start thinking on different terms depending on the type of grief)

1. New roles
2. New priorities
3. New objectives
4. New friends
5. New ideas

The Regaining Confidence phase (in which the person has learned from this grief experience and applies what has been learned)

1. Stronger character is achieved.
2. Energy is boosted.
3. Experience is exchanged with fulfillment.
4. Going through is swap for being capable.

After glancing in my own mind all the possibilities that can happen throughout this grief cycle, one of the biggest concerns I still have is the warning that must be implemented at each phase: Never compare yourself to others. Everything has a cause and effect. There are no accidents, and every comparison we allowed to happen or we make ourselves will get us stuck and paralyzed in that specific phase.

When we know ourselves pretty well, we have no need to compare ourselves, but knowing ourselves well is also understanding how to properly care for our spirit too. I say this because we can easily take good care of our bodies with proper diet, good sleeping habits, and moderate exercises. We can also take good care of our mental faculties and improve our memory with sufficient reading exercises, some mental challenges, and proper rest periods. But one of the attributes we still possess and give less attention to is our spiritual aspect. It is very strange that we don't pay much attention to this attribute, when it is this attribute that gives us the passion and the energy to go after our dreams and the one that is truly going to help us fight the most horrible experiences of our own journey, our darkest hours.

So in closing, I want to recap the whole content of this book in one single paragraph:

> Our darkest hours are excellent periods that take place during our journey to expose where our hearts truly are. If we are holding on to something that we haven't been able to 'let go,' Darkness and Death will show up in a very violent fashion. I am sorry, that's the way they like to introduce themselves. At that point, our situation has been destined to change regardless of whether we cooperate or not, and the heavens will respond according to the attitude we foster. If we strongly and firmly believe we are much bigger than any problem we are facing, or much bigger than anything we haven't been able to let go, our new day (new lifestyle) is about to start. But if we prefer to struggle with Darkness and Death during that midnight hour, please reconsider all the losses we will achieve before the showdown ends.

Biblical References

The items in the list are arranged in the same order they appeared in each chapter (chronological order).

Chapter I: The Principle

Exodus 11:4–7
Exodus 10:21–29
Exodus 11:6–8
Matthew 27:45–46
1 Samuel 17:43, 24:14
Psalm 22:20
2 Peter 2:22
Exodus 22:31
Isaiah 56:10–11
Matthew 7:6
Luke 16:21
Philippians 3:2
Revelation 22:15
Exodus 7–12
Judges 7:19
Judges 6:11–25
Judges 6:13
Judges 6–8
Ruth 3:7–9
Ruth 3:11–13
Book of Ruth

Job 34:20
Job 13:15
Job 42:5
Book of Job
Psalm 119:62
Mark 13:35
Matthew 6:23
Mark 13:5–37
Acts 16:25
Psalm 22:3
Psalm 100:4
Matthew 15:8
Psalm 34:1
John 4:23
Psalm 50:23
Psalm 50:21

Chapter II: Embracing the Process

There are no biblical references in this chapter

Chapter III: Take Time to Listen

1 Kings 19:11–13
1 Kings 19
Genesis 3:8

Chapter IV: Seek Alliance

1 Corinthians 14:10
Matthew 10:16–23

Chapter V: Prepare for Changes

Isaiah 53:3
Isaiah 53:7

Chapter VI: Know Yourself

Luke 6:43–45

Chapter VII: Don't Lose Your Vision

Matthew 6:22–23
Matthew 20:15
1 Corinthians 16:13
Colossians 4:2
1 Thessalonians 5:6
2 Timothy 4:5
Hebrews 13:17
2 Samuel 18:24–27
2 Kings 9:17–20
Ezekiel 33:3
Jeremiah 6:17
Joel 2:1

Chapter VIII: The Struggle Is Not Easy

Romans 8:28

Chapter IX: Remain Friendly

There are no biblical references in this chapter

Chapter X: What Purpose Do
Crises Have in Our Lives?

John 12:24

Chapter XI: Transformation Is Undeniable

Genesis 28:12–19
Genesis 31:3
Genesis 32:24–30
Matthew 5:3

Chapter XII: Don't Neglect Your Own Spirit

Daniel 1:8–19

Chapter XIII: Breakthrough is at Hand

There are no biblical references in this chapter